Passing the Light

A history of the University of Sydney's
International House

Passing the Light

A history of the University of Sydney's International House

from its foundation to its fortieth anniversary 1967–2007

edited by John Gascoigne

 The University of Sydney

First published 2007
by
International House
The University of Sydney
96 City Road
Chippendale NSW 2008
Australia
www.usyd.edu.au/internationalhouse

ISBN 978 1 921364 00 6

Book design: Miguel Yamin - University Publishing Service

Cover design: Miguel Yamin - University Publishing Service

Printed by the University Publishing Service

Compact disc (*inside back cover*) with International House 'year photographs' from 1967 to 2006 and numerous other photographs from the IH archives.

This book is dedicated to all those residents, friends and supporters of International House, University of Sydney, past, present and future who have made possible the "passing of the light"

Contents

The Contributors

Graeme de Graaff was Director of International House from 1965 to 1987. He has been a Fellow of International House since 1986 and is an honorary member of SUIHAA.

John Gascoigne was a resident in 1970, when he was a member of the IHMA committee, and in 1972 (along with his future wife, Kathleen Bock), while he was studying for his second and fourth year of a BA (hons) degree in history. He was a member of the SUIHAA committee in the early 1980s and served as president and as an ex-officio member of the IH Council from 1983 to 1984.

Roger Wescombe was a resident final year undergraduate in 1967, Program Director in 1974 and 1975 and Deputy Director with responsibility for the program of activities from 1982 to 1986.

Brendon Drain was a resident from 1999 to 2000. He was a member of the SUIHAA committee in 2003.

Joan Rowlands (Farrar) was a postgraduate resident in 1970, while undertaking the Diploma of Public Health, and was resident Assistant Director in 1979 and 1980. She has been a member of the SUIHAA committee since 2000, first as Treasurer, then as President, from 2001 to 2003, when she was also an ex-officio member of the IH Council. In 2004 and 2005 she served as Publications Officer on the SUIHAA committee and is still currently a member of it.

Richard Waterhouse was a resident in 1968 and 1969, while he was enrolled for a Master's degree in history. He subsequently abandoned this degree to take up a PhD scholarship at Johns Hopkins University in September 1969. He has taught US and Australian history at the University of Sydney since 1973.

Jessica Carroll emigrated to Australia in 1988 from Dublin, Ireland. She is a graduate of the University of Sydney with a Master's degree in psychology. After serving as Assistant Director from 2000 until 2002, she was appointed Director of the House in June 2002.

Denise North has a BEc (hons) from Sydney University. A Sydney local, she was a resident at International House Sydney in 1980 and 1981, recognising that an honours year might require some work to be done and that IH offered an environment in which that goal might conceivably be achieved. She was appointed to the IH Council in September 2004, serving on the Finance Sub-Committee. She became Chair of Council in December 2006.

David Shannon was a resident from 1967 to 1968. He became a lawyer and spent most of his career as a partner in the international law firm Baker & McKenzie, including sixteen years in the firm's Hong Kong office. He served on the Council of International House in the 1970s and again from 1998 to 2006; he was Chair of Council in 2006.

Graeme de Graaff, founding Director of International House,
University of Sydney, ink drawing by Louis Kahan, 1986
(reproduced by kind permission of Lily Kahan and Viscopy Australia)

Preface and Acknowledgements

Anniversaries are occasions on which to reflect on what has passed and to think anew about the possibilities of the future. International House has always marked its significant birthdays with discussion of what the House stands for and how its ideals and aspirations to ensure 'That fellowship may prevail' may be better achieved. A major part of any such taking-stock is to consider what has been achieved so far and IH's fortieth anniversary is an appropriate occasion to draw together the strands of a history. Such a history aims both to provide a record of the House over the forty years since its foundation in 1967 and, one hopes, also to provide some guidance for the future. For the many whose lives have been intertwined with IH it is a history, too, which forms part of their own history and puts in a more enduring form much of the work that so many have committed to the cause of IH. Indeed, this is a participant history in that the contributors have all been closely involved with IH and chapters have been deliberately allocated to those who have lived through the period about which they write.

This is not an official history in that it does not faithfully follow a view of the institution's history that accords with the views of the management or, indeed, with all those who have devoted time and effort to building up the House. Each chapter is written by an individual whose view of the House has been shaped by their particular circumstances and experiences. Though every attempt has been made to avoid error, different people will recall events in different ways — as happens with any history. Nonetheless, it is hoped that this volume, which is the fruit of considerable archival research, together with attention to oral history, will provide a useful record of International House from its formative years to the present and that it will bring back to life for many individuals their own experience of the House and all it represents.

It provides a sense of the texture of the life over those years — four decades when the pace of change has accelerated ever more. For the House there have been successes aplenty and inevitably also a few failures. As the history spells out, the origins of the International House movement derive from the USA and the 'mother house' in New York (founded in 1924), but transferring the ideals that prompted this movement into the Australian idiom naturally meant that some aspects flourished while others were 'lost in translation'. The ideal of having international students live alongside locals has taken firm root. Well established, too, has been a subsidiary goal: allowing women and men to live under the same roof. The latter is now taken for granted but, as the history makes plain, when the IH was established at Sydney University it was still a novel, daring and somewhat controversial notion.

The aspect of the US movement which travelled less well was the ideal of IH serving as a centre for activities for the international student community more generally. This was a cause to which much effort was devoted, especially in the 1970s and 1990s, as is recounted in these pages. Its lack of success can be attributed to a number of reasons. The Houses in the US were much bigger, with public rooms that could be better separated off from the student residence — an abiding problem with any international centre at IH Sydney was that the needs of a centre and those of the residents (and especially their sense of privacy) were in tension. Also the House in New York, like some other I Houses, was not closely linked to a particular university, whereas the fact that IH Sydney was a part of the University of Sydney meant that students from other universities naturally regarded it as somewhat foreign territory. Perhaps, too, with the passage of time the need for a centre for overseas students has waned as their numbers have grown and, with that, a much readier acceptance of their increasingly prominent role in Australian university life.

When it was established, IH Sydney was unusual in not following the well-established model of the (largely church-affiliated) colleges, but rather that of a hall of residence with its own Council but ultimately under the control of the University. Another theme of IH's history, then, has been its relations with the colleges, which were the Significant Other against which it defined itself. In its earlier days, IH sought kindred spirits at other universities and the (generally) biennial corroborees held in conjunction with the International Houses at the Universities of Melbourne, Queensland, New South Wales and Wollongong provided some sense of solidarity and common purpose. This was the more important since the sporting matches which bound the Sydney colleges together were not IH's 'scene' — postgraduates and foreign students were too busy with their studies to devote much time to rugby training or the cricket nets and the fact that IH was co-educational, when that was unusual, also complicated its sporting profile (though it would have done very well at table tennis).

Gradually, however, the divide between the colleges and IH has become less marked. The colleges themselves have changed and are less traditional in character. Originally IH aimed to provide 'no-frills' service to keep the fees down, but there expectations have risen, while at the colleges the need to reduce costs has meant that IH and the colleges now provide comparable services. The original intention of making IH a largely postgraduate residence has faded somewhat as postgraduates have become increasingly unwilling to live in student residences. Indeed the flight from institutions, which is a feature of our age, has meant that all forms of halls of residence or colleges are facing something of a dearth of applicants as students make their own arrangements. In response, universities have moved to provide other forms of accommodation, such as student villages, where students cook for themselves and where the communal life, basic to a hall of residence, has largely receded. All of this has further diminished any sharp line of division between International House and the colleges; they now seem to have much more in common than was readily apparent when IH was founded. One reflection of this is that IH's involvement in some forms of intercollegiate activity, such as debating, has waxed and the need for mutual International House solidarity in the form of the interstate corroborees has waned.

The changing fortunes of student accommodation have had their effects on the composition of the House. When it began, the aim was to have equal numbers of overseas and Australian students. Ideally, too, the goal was to mirror the student population of the University: one-third women and two-thirds men. Parity in these numbers was gradually achieved, as women came to form at least half of the student body of the University by the mid-seventies. What would have seemed surprising, however, in the early days of the House is the fact that it has become increasingly difficult to achieve the target of half the residents being Australian — reflecting that more general flight from institutionalised student accommodation over recent years. In part, this is related to rising running costs, for student residences are labour-intensive. It is, however, also a social trend, captured in the title of the book by the influential US sociologist, Robert Putnam, *Bowling Alone: The Collapse and Revival of American Community* (New York, 2000), which takes the fact that people are less inclined even to join bowling teams as symptomatic of a general shunning of institutions.

But, in its forty years, IH has already seen these and other social trends come and go and, no doubt, will see many more such in the years to come. It weathered the student upheavals of the sixties and seventies with remarkable ease and indeed seemed to draw strength and energy from the idealism of that age. In the 1980s and 1990s it has had to deal with a university climate in which the user-pays principle has become more and more pronounced — an environment which has led to a considerable expansion in the number of overseas students which, in turn, has made IH's role one of significance. Its building program over the years has been that of an institution ready to grasp the opportunity to grow and diversify, providing new niches such as the married accommodation in the Maze apartments. Though IH now seems too landlocked to grow outwards much more, it continues to adapt its existing buildings to new uses. The original residents would be surprised, for example, to find that that the once-neglected roof top is now regularly used for social occasions at which guests look down on the city arrayed beneath them.

The House has adapted, too, to the changing character of the society around it and in some ways has taken a lead. Women have always played a major role in the House's leadership, as instanced by the enormous impact of Rosalie McCutcheon, the House's first Deputy Director; and of recent years the House has had two successive female Directors, Ruth Shatford and Jessica Carroll. One subject that looms large in these pages is food — a fundamental concern for any institution (particularly as grumbling about its inadequacies provides a strong bonding experience). Though it is hard to please everyone all the time (especially given the budget constraints), IH's cuisine has more and more reflected the multicultural character of the institution.

The development of the Log Cabin in the Belanglo State Forest is an instance of IH's innovative outreach — and the increasing sophistication of the facilities there perhaps an example of the receding Australian bush legend, as bucket showers and pit-toilets have become less and less congenial. IH and the ideals for which it stands still can energise and change lives and, in new circumstances with new challenges, will carry forward the work of the last forty years that this publication chronicles.

It is with pleasure that I thank the many people that have brought this volume to pass. In the first place, Ian G. Hudson AM, one of the House's great patrons, provided the wherewithal that made the venture possible. Jessica Carroll saw the need for the work and she and, while she was on maternity leave, Keith Smith kept up the momentum of the project, ably aided by Claudia Morales.

The long-serving committee consisted of the contributors to this work (London-based Brendon Drain joined us in spirit), along with Peter Lean, Gwen Ng and Jean Cooney (who copy-edited the volume, the fourth time she and I have worked on a book together). The index we owe to Alan Walker (the fifth publication he has indexed for me). My thanks, too, to Graeme de Graaff and Youngsok Song for devoting much time and effort to organising the pictures for the book and the accompanying compact disc; and to Melba Studios, Sydney, for their kind co-operation for providing negatives of most of the year photos, of which they hold the copyright.

Without the efficient services of Jackie Hartley who, over some four months, reorganised the archives and provided an invaluable catalogue of their contents, together with IH material in the University archives, this book would scarcely have been possible; indeed, any future historian of the House should begin by consulting these catalogues, which are kept on file at the House. I should also like to pay tribute to the bygone work of Rosemary Berrick who, in the first decades of the House's history, served as honorary archivist and to whom those (such as myself) who wrote on those years owe a considerable debt for her work in preserving and organising much valuable material.

As editor, it is appropriate that I should conclude by thanking the contributors, who willingly gave a great deal of their time to the demanding task of writing the chapters which make up this book. Such willingness to serve is an indication of the lasting impact of International House and what it stands for.

John Gascoigne
Sydney, March 2007

Chapter One
The Foundation Years
Graeme de Graaff

The massive stone pile of Queen's College, my undergraduate home at the University of Melbourne, began life humbly in the mid-nineteenth century sheltering a dozen country boys and a couple of candidates for the Methodist ministry.

A predominantly working-class church could ill afford it, but sacrifices had to be made because the University of Melbourne, like its Sydney counterpart, began in the period of liberal secular enlightenment. The study of religion was to be left to others and there was jealousy between the branches of the church. So, in Melbourne and Sydney the secular university was bordered by grants of land to the churches. There they built their colleges, affiliated with, but not part of, the university proper. And there they did, and sometimes still do, study religion and theology and provide additional tutorials in university subjects. But while some even cater for non-resident students, their core activity has become to provide board and lodging adjacent to the campus.

My college in Oxford began in the thirteenth century with a dozen Scottish lads. They were enjoying the beneficence of John Balliol and his wife Dervorguilla (parents of John Balliol, King of Scotland), who hoped by this work of charity to offset some less respectable ventures and so improve their chances in the afterlife. Balliol was probably the earliest of the Oxford colleges which were modelled on religious communities. The university was a sort of administrative federation of the colleges and it was in the latter that all the teaching took place.

International House in Melbourne, the earliest of the Australian Houses, was a 1950s' response to the wave of Colombo Plan students, chiefly from Asia, and Fulbright students from the USA and Europe, coinciding with the development of postgraduate courses. The initiative of a group of Indian students was taken up by the Student Representative Council. Rotary clubs were involved in fund-raising. So were Melbourne University students and staff. I remember being unable to exit lectures without first contributing two shillings at the door. At the Union Theatre audiences were obliged to buy coffee and cake at inflated rates, served by the Society of University Women working for International House. I remember a row of pennies snaking for hundreds of yards around the main quadrangle. The Melbourne International House sought 'to advance the goals of cross-cultural peace, friendship

*Graeme de Graaff and Harry Edmonds at the 50th anniversary of
New York I House, New York, 1977*

and harmony. To this day we strive to fulfil these goals in line with our motto of *fraternitas* (brotherhood)'.

That Melbourne motto acknowledges the first serious International House in the world, for 'That brotherhood may prevail' is the motto of International House adjacent to Columbia University in New York. The New York House was the brainchild of Harry Edmonds, a 26-year-old YMCA and Student Christian Movement worker at Columbia University in 1909. On a frosty morning on the steps of the library, Harry greeted two Chinese students with a cheerful, 'Hello, great day!' They stopped and chatted. On parting they said, 'Thank you for talking with us. You are the first person other than an official who has spoken to us since arriving here'. He gave them his address and suggested that they might come to supper the following Sunday.

They came. Because they were Chinese and polite, they brought a couple of friends with them. It went well, so they came back a few weeks later. And because they were polite they brought a few more friends with them. After a time the Edmonds hired the local church hall to accommodate the Sunday Supper guests. They invited some of their American friends to join them.

The isolation of the foreign students worried Harry and he regretted that American students were missing the enrichment of association with these people from different cultures. The Sunday supper gatherings were formalised into the 'Cosmopolitan Club'. Edmonds dreamt of finding a house, as a group of Quakers had done in Washington, where foreign and American students could live together and move beyond polite friendship to real understanding. Members of the Dodge and Carnegie families supported the Cosmopolitan Club as it moved from one rented premises to another, providing accommodation for a handful of resident students. But it was John D. Rockefeller Jr who in 1924 responded magnificently to the challenge. He financed a splendid building on Riverside Drive, which accommodated 500 students, because Rockefeller's hotel advisers said that was the minimum necessary for economic survival. It was Rockefeller who asked that above the main door there should be carved the words: 'That Brotherhood May Prevail'. And to show he really meant it, Rockefeller built comparable Houses in Chicago and Berkeley in the USA, and a whole village of them in Paris.

When I met him at the 50th anniversary of the New York House, Harry Edmonds revised the details of the story of the beginnings of IH, but he confirmed that it was indeed that encounter on the steps of the library which set him on the path which led to the foundation of the Cosmopolitan Club and International House.

There was, I believe, a gentle hint from Sydney that the Rockefellers might be interested in the antipodes. They were pleased that the idea had reached so far — and one of them visited years later. While there was no Rockefeller money, there was a strong ideological link from New York and Berkeley to Sydney. There was no Rockefeller for Sydney, nor was there anyone like him.

Our House at Sydney University did not suddenly and magically appear with doors open for the first 120 students in 1967. That great day may have been magical but it was preceded by years of very down-to-earth activity. There had been years of dreaming, forming committees, raising funds, losing heart, starting again, passing the baton to fresh enthusiasts, struggling along, stalling again — until finally after some fifteen years the House was a reality. It all started in Sydney University's centenary year. The University needed academic staff; it needed buildings; it needed laboratory equipment; it needed a new library. And it needed student accommodation. So in 1952 the Lord Mayor's Hostel Fund was established. Some £2300 must have been raised, because that amount eventually found its way into an International House fund. But the word 'international' is not to be found in the vague documentation, nor any clue as to why the idea apparently just faded away.

In 1954 the secretary of the Overseas Students' Bureau, Margaret Briggs, prepared a report on the need for an International House. In

July that year the OSB publicly screened a film, *Neither East nor West*, made by the director of the Methodist International House in London. By September of 1955 the Bureau was happy to announce that 'the Students Representative Council had accepted responsibility for (the campaign) on the student level'.

We know of the Lord Mayor's non-existent hostel only because Betty Battle, lecturer in Social Work and a member of the Sydney Chapter of the 'International House Association', remembered that fund-raising had taken place. The International House Association was the alumni organisation for the Rockefeller Houses, financed and managed through the New York House. The Sydney Chapter of the association believed that there should be an I House on the University of Sydney campus. Three active alumni in Sydney were involved in our House: Harold Wyndham, Director General of Education in New South Wales, Hans Freeman, reader in Chemistry in the University, and Betty Battle. The two men appear again in this book. As Betty retired and returned to Melbourne before the House opened, however, she comes into the story only because in July 1959 the Student Representative Council's efforts at raising money for an International House needed administrative support. At Betty Battle's suggestion, the University, after taking legal advice, made the Lord Mayor's Hostel funds available to the SRC to cover the operating costs of the International House Appeal.

In February that year the Vice-Chancellor, Professor Stephen Roberts, reported to the University Senate that the SRC Committee was being set up to acquire a site and subsequently administer an International House and that they had requested the Senate to nominate a representative on their Committee. The Senate appointed the University Assistant Principal, W. Harold Maze. There might still have been years of labour and angst ahead, but from the time of Maze's appointment, the gods would have known that an International House was a certainty. The International House Trustees held their first meeting in May 1959.

Harold Maze headed the team which saw the University recover from the neglect of, first, the Depression years and, then, the Second World War. It was a period of frenetic expansion and building. Maze was the son of Irish immigrants (who carefully never quite lost his own slight brogue), a Fort Street School boy who had worked his way through his Geography degree. A lecturer in Geography, he had calculated the age of his professor and the opportunities for promotion, and decided to step sideways. He became Assistant Registrar and rapidly advanced to Registrar, then Assistant Principal and finally Deputy Principal.

Travelling the world studying the post-war trends in universities, Maze translated what he found into his contribution to the development of the University of Sydney. The University's move into Darlington was his single biggest project and happily its main road now bears his name, as does the final wing built at International House.

Maze sympathised with the student drive to have an International House. He was encouraged by some of the Sydney academic staff who were alumni of the American Houses. And he was content to be seen as not a great admirer of the existing Sydney colleges. When visiting universities he always stayed if he could on campus, preferably in a student hall. He stayed in Berkeley and New York International Houses. He became enthusiastic about International Houses and developed a firm friendship with Sheridan Warrick, the Director at Berkeley, and Howard Cook, the President at New York. He stored away everything he could collect about these successful, established Houses which he so much enjoyed. There were even breakfast menus in the material that I inherited from him.

The Menzies era brought a great advance in the development of universities in Australia following the release of the federal government's *Murray Report* in 1957, which had stressed the importance of university residences for overseas students. Old universities were rescued from the dismal pre-war dilapidation, new universities were established, and postgraduate study became a reality without graduates having to head off for the United Kingdom or the United States. Student residences also benefited and by the mid-sixties every residential college in Australia would either just be starting or have just completed a new building project. With one state pound of funding and two commonwealth pounds given for every pound raised by a college, it was too good an opportunity to be missed. But still there was not enough accommodation at Sydney.

There was enthusiastic SRC activity in that year of 1959. In July the proceeds of the annual Commem Day (student festival) went directly to the International House Appeal. By August there was a draft constitution including provision for managing the House. (There was a slight hiatus the next month when it was simply reported that the minutes of the Appeal Committee had been received. The chief business of that SRC meeting was its prescient admiration for the skills of one Clive James whom they authorised to produce a literary news sheet.)

In August the Senate agreed with the Vice-Chancellor's proposal that the 'University Hostel for University Students and Friendship Centre' could be recognised as a college within the University. But in December that year Maze advised the Senate, when requesting that Sydney University set aside a site for its International House, that the SRC appeal was for two Houses, the second one being for the new

L to r: Sir Charles McDonald, Chancellor of the University of Sydney, Mr W. Edmund Manson, Hong Kong Trade Commissioner, Sir Bernard Freeman, Justice John Clancy, Chancellor of the University of New South Wales, at 96 City Road, Chippendale, 1965

University of New South Wales. The Senate agreed — a landmine agreement that lay dormant for years. However, for the present, progress seemed to have been made when, in October 1960, the Senate agreed to Maze's proposal that, in the new Darlington extension area, sites should be reserved for a Church of England Women's College, for four tower residences to house 800 students, and for International House.

This was Maze's response to the more limited vision of the SRC Appeal Committee. For, buoyed by a massive donation of £4000 from the Malaysian Government, the SRC Committee was eyeing an available large house across the Harbour in the Northbridge area. They had the English Methodist International House model in mind. Harold Maze did not like the idea. It was too small. It was on the wrong side of the Harbour for either university. He urged the committee to hold off. He knew that there was a possibility of Rotary becoming involved.

In 1962 the SRC included in their submission to the newly formed Universities Commission (established by the Commonwealth Government in response to the seminal *Murray Report*) their support for the foundation of International House, claiming that they had initiated the move which had 'received immediate support from the University who agreed to supply the land', and indicating that action was being taken to raise funds towards the estimated cost of £300,000.

But from 1960 onwards, the SRC's fund-raising efforts appear to have petered out. The dusty archives of their correspondence record only the wistful demands of a series of university clerks that the SRC Committee should please abide by the agreement with the University and submit the required audited accounts.

The campaign moved to a new level with the entry of Rotary. Individual Rotarians had on several occasions talked of the need for an International House. As far back as 1956, the Rotary clubs of the 29th District (later designated District 275) began planning a District conference to be held in the Great Hall of Sydney University. The President of the Rotary Club of South Sydney, Ron Moran, discussed with the Chancellor in a general way the possibility of Rotary sponsorship of a hall of residence for foreign students. When the conference was held in the 1956–57 year, the District Governor, (Sir) George Proud, asked in his concluding speech in what way Rotary might assist the University. The Chancellor, Sir Charles Bickerton Blackburn, needing no further invitation, stressed the great need for student residential accommodation.

Apart from an occasional surfacing, the idea of an International House lay dormant in Rotary for five years, but Rotary work with international students did not. After his term as District Governor, Dr Geoff Howe remembered Sir Charles Bickerton Blackburn's response to the earlier offer of help for the University and he raised the matter with an informal group at the District conference. The incoming District Governor in 1961, Sleath Lowrey, formed a committee and the fateful decision was made to make the raising of funds for International House a major project in the District.

The University of Sydney welcomed Rotary's approach. The inaugural meeting of the 'Universities [sic] International Houses [sic] Appeal' was held in the Vice-Chancellor's room on 12 July 1961. Critically, Harold Maze became Executive Secretary of this committee at its second meeting. But at one stroke the half-marathon had become a full marathon. The Vice-Chancellor of the University of New South Wales was a Rotarian. He had called in the old undertaking that both universities would be provided for. Rotary found itself committed to raising £200,000!

There were two things about this decision, both of which were to cause problems in the Rotary community. The first was that this would be a huge project, with the target of £200,000 to be matched three pounds for one by the federal and state governments. It could not be done by one Rotary club, but this would be the first time in Australia that all the clubs in the Rotary District would be asked to join together on a single project. Second, there was a tradition in Rotary that any project which started in one Rotary year should be finished in that year. There was no way that that would be possible with this one. To compound the problem, the Vice-Chancellor of the University of New South Wales had a different idea for student accommodation. He envisaged a block of small rooms, let at £1 per week, with no common facilities — the residents would find their meals in the student Union. He was not interested in an international student centre.

Sleath Lowrey spoke about the project at all his official visits to Rotary clubs during his year of office, urging support for this venture which so neatly matched the fourth part of the object of Rotary, which is to foster international understanding, goodwill and peace. Sydney Rotarian, Lyn Knight, principal of a professional fund-raising company, volunteered his services and dedicated Rotarians met with him on Sundays at the Fisher Library to be trained for their tasks. That was to tackle the big prospects. All the usual Rotary Club fund-raising activities were also employed:

> We have had Raffles, Bowls Days, Golf Days, Barbecues, Carnivals, Special Film Shows, Musical Evenings, Concerts, Progressive Dinners, Theatre Parties, Music Hall Nights, Balls, Dances, Sale of Character Drawings, Fashion Parades, Sale of Christmas Cards, Car Races, Boat Picnics, Olympic Sports Days, Doll Displays, Garden Inspections, and even an 81-year-old Hurstville Rotarian collecting scrap metal which he sold for £50,

— thus wrote Bruce Smith (President of Parramatta Rotary Club, who would become the longest serving Board member of the University of NSW International House). And some unusual big District activities were organised, such as the mammoth television auction on Channel 7 with a target of £30,000, when 255 lots of the most assorted goods and objects were bid for and sold. The Sydney Club, after some opposition, doubled its luncheon fee from ten shillings to one pound, the extra charge being donated to the IH appeal. The tactic was recommended to other clubs in the District.

Fund-raising proved to be hard going. There was little public support in the suburbs for universities or university students, for, despite the depressed state of the former, which had been identified by the *Murray Report*, they were seen as elitist and university students as privileged and overindulged. 'The University is full anyway', was a comment that occasionally varied some muttered trace of a 'White Australia' sentiment.

The appeal dragged on. If relations between the two universities and their Vice-Chancellors had been cool to start with, the International Houses Appeal did not do much to promote even inter-university understanding. While the University of Sydney at its own expense provided space and staff to service the Rotary appeal, the University of New South Wales only complained that more donations were earmarked for Sydney than for New South Wales — inevitably, as the newer university did not have an old-established alumni base to call upon. Rotarian Seymour Shaw at the 1966 District 268 conference made an impassioned call to arms:

> We believe that the completion of these International Houses is a tremendous challenge to every one of us and to the people of this State... We accept this challenge, and we ask you to support us now, just in the remaining stages, so that this can be accomplished — the greatest thing, I believe, that has ever been attempted by Rotary in Australia. Fellows, let's to our task with high resolve!

By the time Ian Hudson became District Governor, some of his fellow Rotarians were contemplating the committee's withdrawal from its commitment to the University of New South Wales. Hudson insisted that the reputation of Rotary was at stake and urged the clubs in his District and the newly emerged District 268 to finish the task. He and his friend, Seymour Shaw, set off, at their own expense, to Hong Kong to raise funds. There were many students coming to Australia from the then Crown Colony and there were also wealthy companies and individuals there. Hudson and Shaw met with a modest response. Meanwhile the University of Sydney, irreversibly committed to its House, proceeded to work out how it would handle a shortfall in funding.

At the University of Sydney, a Provisional Board of Management was set up. It met first in February 1964. Appropriate sub-committees were established. Lieutenant-General Sir John Northcott, retired Governor of New South Wales, was the chairman. His deputy, who would take over when Sir John died in 1966, was His Honour Justice Charles McLelland, Chief Judge in Equity. The University was well represented: Sir Charles Bickerton Blackburn, the old Chancellor who had first sown the seeds with Rotary was there; the Vice-Chancellor, Emeritus Professor Sir Stephen Roberts (just visible in a perpetual cloud of cigarette smoke and confessing that he would be happier when International House was already a subject for historical study); Major-General I. N. Dougherty (Deputy Chancellor); Mr Harold Maze (Assistant Principal); Sir Charles McDonald (Fellow of Senate); Emeritus Professor A. P. Elkin (Fellow

The Provisional Board of Management, 1965; standing, l to r:
Mr Harold Maze, Emeritus Professor A. P. Elkin, Mr Sleath Lowrey,
Mr J. O. Fairfax, Emeritus Professor Sir Stephen Roberts,
Mr Seymour Shaw, Dr Geoff Howe, Miss Doreen Langley,
Sir Charles McDonald, Mr Fred Kirby; seated, l to r:
Mr Bernard Freeman, Lt-Gen. Sir John Northcott,
Sir Charles Bickerton Blackburn, Justice Charles McLelland

of Senate) and Mr (later Sir) Noel Foley (Fellow of Senate and Director of British Tobacco). The media were represented by the generous benefactors, Sir Frank Packer (Chair of Australian Consolidated Press) and Mr J. O. Fairfax (Director of John Fairfax and a Balliol man).

The Rotarians who had worked so hard for so long were represented by Mr (later Sir) Bernard Freeman (Chair and Managing Director of Metro Goldwyn Mayer); Mr (later Sir) Theo Kelly (Chair and Managing Director of Woolworths, Treasurer of the Appeal Committee); Dr G. L. Howe; Mr Sleath Lowrey (Managing Director of O. J. Williams); and Mr E. Seymour Shaw (Chairman of Hunt Bros). Dr (later Sir) Harold Wyndham missed the first meeting, but was one of the most active members of that Board. Mr F. W. Kirby attended as Maze's assistant. And, yes, there was a woman: Miss Doreen Langley, Principal of Women's College at the University of Sydney and regarded in the academic world as the Australian expert on students in residence. She was there because Maze valued her knowledge and her wisdom, not as the token woman as one might have suspected from the wording of the constitution which later set up the permanent Council of International

House. For there, having provided that there would be 'representatives of Rotary' on the Council, the paragraph concluded with the words 'and at least one woman'.

Committees were established to draft a constitution and regulations; to plan the building; to manage the finances; while the committee to appoint a Director was instructed to meet as soon as possible. That might seem strange, given that there was still doubt about the funding and the opening of Sydney University's International House was at least two years away.

On Harold Maze's staff were architects and planners. But he believed that the brief for the mushrooming university buildings should, if possible, be first written by a client, who should then oversee the project through the turmoil of changes that budget and regulations would entail. If there were no existing department head, as in a new project like IH, then one should be appointed. The Vice-Chancellor, albeit with a grumble about 'what's that man manipulating this time?', literally 'put his tick' on Maze's memorandum.

The minutes of the second meeting of the Provisional Board reveal that there had been a lot of committee activity since meeting number one. The Project Planning Committee set out that:

> The concept of an International House implies a residential institution on the campus or within the university enclave designed to meet a special purpose; it is inherently different from a regular hall of residence. The House will have two main purposes. On the one hand it should provide for strangers in a strange land, facilities for living and study as individuals under reasonably comfortable conditions. On the other, it should provide opportunities for easy contact between individuals and groups of overseas students with Australian students. In regards to the latter objective, particular significance is to be attached to the provision both for eating facilities communal and incidental and places for social intercourse, recreation and conversation.

The Committee for the Appointment of the Director reported that he would be the Executive Officer of the Council and the CEO of the House, would be appointed for three years and would be non-resident. (There was little space for family living on the triangular site. Doreen Langley had argued that the University should buy a house in Glebe for the Director, but Maze thought that was an unnecessary expense. He himself travelled from Roseville each day. What was so special about a head of college, particularly as International House would be occupied by 'mature students who would need no resident policeman'?) The committee pronounced that the Director was to

> manage International House; to assist, advise and exercise general superintendence over resident and non-resident students; to develop the House as a centre for the interchange of ideas between Australian and overseas students and encourage the cultural and social life of the House. In addition, the Director will maintain liaison with Rotary, which is sponsoring the Universities International House Appeal and has undertaken to continue its assistance in the working of the House... [The Director] will arrange for tutorial help when needed.

Lest applicants got too carried away, the advertisement included the information that the salary would be £3245 and noted (or should that be 'warned'?) that as at May only £135,000 of the £200,000 had been raised by the Rotary appeal and that only half of this amount would be available for Sydney University.

Optimistically, the information for applicants returned to the things that mattered:

> The purpose of the project is to provide accommodation for approximately 150 resident students, male and female, half of them being Australian students and the other half from overseas. It is proposed that International House will also be used as a centre for non-resident members under conditions to be determined. There will be dining, reading, social, tutorial and other amenities for facilitating the interchange of ideas and cultures, to the benefit of both local and overseas peoples. There will also be provision for accommodation of special visitors. It is hoped that the house will promote friendly relations between peoples of all races and especially between Australians and S. E. Asians in view of the predominance of that area in our overseas student numbers.

By 1965 the appeal was drawing to a close. The first Director had been appointed, paid for by the University and slipped onto the Deputy Principal's establishment, even though there would be no students for another couple of years. It was hoped that he might do his bit in finishing off the appeal. A foreigner in Sydney and a born non-fund-raiser, he was not much use even though he talked to every Rotary Club in the state, carting with him a beautifully made model of buildings which we were still not sure could be built. He was talking to a weary audience. Radio interviews and chat shows brought in little money but did attract curious innuendo about what was going on, or about to go on up at the University now — with men and women, and students at that, living in the one college! Wesley College bravely 'went co-ed' the next year, and that took the heat off the as yet unfinished International House. At the third meeting of the Board on 23 March 1965 it was clear that the fund-raising was stalling. It was decided to seek the permission of the Senate to borrow for the shortfall. A somewhat surprised new Director was then introduced!

I had not been the first choice of either the Vice-Chancellor or Harold Maze. Maze had planned originally to emphasise the non-collegiate and 'modern' nature of the project by having an 'Officer-in-Charge'. Having lost the minor battle of the name, he had surveyed the considerable number of applications and been in favour of a New Zealand non-academic who looked like a solid no-nonsense administrator. However, in one of his rare misjudgements Maze had put Doreen Langley, a college principal and a member of the University Senate, on the selection committee. As was her wont, Doreen Langley had conferred with Davis McCaughey, Master of Ormond College in Melbourne. Together over the years these two had taken a keen interest in who would be appointed as their colleagues in the small national clique, the Heads of Colleges Association. They had decided that I should not be in Queen's and that I should be in International House.

I had come almost by accident to find myself in Stephen Roberts's room, being interviewed by him, Maze, Doreen Langley, Sir Harold Wyndham, anthropologist A. P. Elkin and Sir Bernard Freeman. I wanted to be Master of Queen's College. My sponsors on that Council thought that as I was already the resident Vice-Master, my chances as the home-grown applicant, especially one tainted (in the view of the theological bloc) by being a senior lecturer in Philosophy, would be enhanced if Queen's had to compete for me with other offers. I dutifully applied for the headship of three other institutions. I was offered each of them: but not Queen's.

When I hesitated to name a date for moving to Sydney, as Maze pressed me to do in his room after lunch with the committee, he was irritated. I discovered later that he knew all about my other irons in the fire and, as he thought I was negotiating, he suggested a higher starting salary!

Maze need not have worried about my accepting the job. In the few hours in Sydney I had caught his enthusiasm for this new project.

Even though on a tour of the allocated site with Robert Bland and Max Jackson, the two architects on his staff, I had been shocked at how tiny and noisy it was, I had been infected by the air of lively rebuilding and optimism which pervaded the University of Sydney.

I arrived back at Melbourne airport that evening at the same time as my wife, Lauris Elms, was returning from a concert engagement in New Zealand and in the car on the way home we decided to move to Sydney. My wife had found life less than exciting in Melbourne compared with her time as Principal Contralto at the Royal Opera House in London before I persuaded her to accompany me back to Australia. As the Music Department of the ABC and the Elizabethan Opera were both based in Sydney and as interstate parochialism still prevailed, she was happy to make the move. The University would pay my salary and expenses and provide office space until such time as the House could manage alone.

I found myself in an office on the corridor overlooking the Vice-Chancellor's quadrangle. It belonged to Graham Scarlett, a father figure from the first moment, the sometime student adviser who was a general assistant to Harold Maze. Scarlett said little unless asked. He observed and privately analysed much. After the new very youthful-looking Master of Wesley and I had been nattering for a couple of hours one day, Scarlett was unable to resist the comment that heads of colleges appeared to be appointed straight from school these days. It did not occur to me at the time that he meant both of us.

Maze's secretary asked what I would like. While I was still thinking, she produced a stack of foolscap pads and a supply of biros and pencils. Scarlett said I would need a budget. Three budgets in fact. One to finish the building; one to furnish it; and one to operate it! Those pads stayed with me for the next two years. Pocket calculators did not exist and if there was a mechanical adding machine on the corridor nobody told me of it. So three blankets per person for 120 students at £3/6/2 each, was multiplied out (remembering that there were 12 pence to a shilling, and 20 shillings to a pound), entered in the column and, page by page, added manually. When an estimate for either the number of teaspoons or their price was seen to be inaccurate the whole thing had to be laboriously recalculated. As I mused with the Rector of St John's, driving home from a philosophy conference in Canberra, about what staff we would need, he looked a bit vague and said that I had better have a talk with his college's matron. She drafted a plan in no time.

Another member of Maze's staff was Fred Kirby who handed over to me the secretarial side of the Appeal Committee and the Provisional Board of Management and its committees. A senior administrator, Fred Kirby, had cradled the IH project from its rocky beginnings through all the uncertainties to this stage. He had become personally involved with everybody connected with the appeal, liaising with the various groups and organisations of overseas students, and his wisdom was generously available. So, at that third meeting of the Board, my first, I found myself taking the minutes and I presented my first version of our operating estimates and the variations which would follow if we had to reduce the number of bedrooms.

By the Board's fourth meeting in September we had been through much hard thinking. The Planning Sub-committee was Harold Wyndham's province. As the author of the NSW Education Department's *Wyndham Report* (which had brought in the six-year secondary school syllabus), he was strong on planning. An alumnus of the New York IH, he was also strong in support of our aims.

From that committee came the principles on which the House opened two years later. There were to be resident and non-resident members. As postgraduate studies were in the ascendant, it was assumed that more and more of the overseas students would be senior people. The House should therefore not restrict them with rules and regulations of the boarding school type. Half the residents should be Australian. One-third should be female (the University proportion at the time). No one national group should predominate. Years of residence should be limited. And, most important of all, the program of activities should be what distinguished International House from other residential colleges: the program should ensure that national cliques did not develop and that opportunity was provided for cross-cultural exchange and understanding. So important was this seen to be that an ominous proviso was written in: should funds not be sufficient to build for the planned number of residents, the latter would be reduced while the program centre should proceed as planned. The emphasis in this report on the International Centre, as distinct from the dormitory, was partly a result of the general concern at the direction being taken by the thinking of the University of New South Wales.

The Building Sub-committee was already struggling with the possibility that the building would have to be smaller. Walter Bunning's design of rotunda, bridge and eight-floor dormitory had solved some of the problems of the small site and of the dual centre and residence. But it did not easily lend itself to reduction or to being built part now and more later. A floor was pulled off the rotunda; a banana-shaped building was tried in lieu of the rotunda; floors were lopped off the dormitory section. Nothing really worked. And the Universities Commission, which held the purse strings for the three-to-one contribution from government, had their own formulae for what common areas were acceptable for a particular number of beds. They were not interested in our non-resident International Student Centre and bluntly told us to get rid of the facilities for non-resident students.

Having taken note of all this, the Provisional Board at that September meeting recommended to Senate that the University accept the tender of E. A. Watts for £290,846, and approve the Board's borrowing £50,000. It noted that the Director, on the Board's behalf, would submit the revised scheme to the Australian Universities Commission in Canberra with a detailed breakdown of the costs, which would show that a hall of residence for 120 students was being built for exactly £300,000 (which fitted the approved AUC formula). He would argue for the right of International House to combine with this hall of residence, at its own expense, dining and common room facilities for non-resident students and additional resident students to be accommodated in future buildings. The Board clearly believed that, although I might not have achieved much as a fund-raiser, I had great ability in argument.

The Commission was persuaded. And thanks to the media families' donations, Walter Bunning's original model was left intact. Except, that is, for the deletion of the charming rooftop apartment and garden designed for the resident Assistant Director. It was not the Universities Commission which said no to that, but the fact that it was deemed a ninth floor and would therefore entail the installation a fire sprinkler system for the whole building. Disappointing as this deletion was, we had cause often over the next two decades to be glad there was no such system. The fire alarms malfunctioned with monotonous regularity. Had the sprinklers sprayed water throughout the House on each such occasion wet suits and waterproof textbooks would have been required by all residents.

As it was, there were indeed early water problems. Apart from leaking showers, the bane of every student residence I have known, the domestic-size hot water units installed on each floor were unreliable. When one actually burst, flooding the corridor and adjacent rooms with near-boiling water, residents leapt on their beds or chairs and yelled for help. A senior Japanese professor padded along the corridor, turned off the water supply and padded back to his room to the silent amazement of the young. He was heard to mutter something about the difference between Christianity and Zen. But that incident belongs in another chapter.

What does belong here is the explanation of why there were separate hot water units. We had decided that unlike the colleges, which had to close their kitchens and their boilers during the long vacation leaving their few overseas and postgraduate students either to move out or camp with inadequate facilities, we would stay open all year round. This meant ensuring that, as we would be far from fully occupied during the summer, facilities could be provided in sections.

Back at the planning stage, there were some easier problems to solve in the meantime. Walter Bunning's annotation on the drawings could be changed to better reflect our planning. His 'Senior Common Room' became a 'Sitting Room' for, after all, we were all going to be senior. It was a beautiful room off the rotunda stairwell on level 2, twenty years later metamorphosed into two sets of toilets, alas. The dais for a high table could be deleted, as no diner would be higher than any other.

I had wanted to continue some academic work and this had been readily agreed to. When I arrived in Sydney, I was asked by David Armstrong, my ex-Melbourne colleague who had just taken up the Challis Chair in Sydney, to fill in for a lecturer whose appointment he was having difficulty in getting approved. I found myself for a time with a lecturing load close to full-time, which nobody had intended or approved. There began a pattern which lasted for the next twenty years, as stages 2, 3 and 4 of the building were planned, funded and built. From meetings with architects, builders or money people, I would run across the campus to a lecture theatre. Catching my breath was not too difficult; switching my brain from the details of a building expansion joint passing impossibly through the middle of a row of toilets to the contradictions in the Lockean Social Contract took longer. On the day when I stood at the lectern and opened my lecture note folder to reveal only architectural estimates, I gave an interesting lecture.

Harold Maze organised Fulbright funds so that I could visit the Rockefeller Houses, and the British Council and French government paid money to demonstrate that they were doing good things too for their foreign students. I set off in the summer vacation. Demolition of the old City Road terrace houses and pub was completed and in the foundations already poured we could see the distinctive shape of the House. It was a matter of waiting now. I did wonder what would happen if I discovered on my travels that we had got the building completely wrong.

If Maze and his crew had enthused me about International Houses, my first hours in the Berkeley House with its wonderful architecture and vibrating life completed my conversion. That night there was a Sunday Supper in the Auditorium. Harold and Molly Maze were guests over the other side of the hall, our paths curiously having crossed. I sat with a couple of ex-students of mine from Queen's! But it was the unfamiliar and the new that excited me. Sherry Warrick, the Director, and his wife,

Betsey, unpatronisingly took me under their wing — they are friends forty years later. Irene Prescott, the dynamic, high-powered Program Director, spent days with me. (On her retirement she came at her own expense to Sydney to help us.)

Visits to the Chicago, Philadelphia, Washington and New York Houses followed; in Paris, the Cité Universitaire and the student residences in the French provinces; and in London the remarkable International Student House in the six converted Nash Terraces presided over by Mary Trevellyan (who also came to us in Sydney to make sure we were getting it right). Up and down the country I visited the Methodist International Houses and learned how not to do it on a shoestring.

Back in Sydney it was time to move into a terrace house in City Road to keep close tabs on the progress of our building. Rosalie McCutcheon joined me there. I had first met Rosalie in 1958 after a Student Christian Movement conference in Edinburgh. At midnight outside St Giles High Kirk to our embarrassment she gathered up the few of us Australians to dance in celebration. Her nephew had been with me in Queen's and the McCutcheon firm had been the college's architects. Rosalie was between jobs, having finished her work with the World University Service before starting as resident Student Christian Movement Secretary at Sydney University. Coincidentally, when she took up her job at Sydney she was allotted an office in the Institute Building next door to Miss Reid, who was employed to handle the Rotary appeal. After her years in the World University Service, assisting displaced students and academics from Europe to make their way in Australia, Rosalie was already an enthusiastic advocate for IH.

On our way to Sydney from Melbourne in January 1965, we stopped off at the Student Christian Movement Conference at Frensham School in Mittagong. Rosalie was part of the Frensham family, having been the first Head of Gib Gate, the junior school. We found ourselves the last to leave the dining hall one day. She said she knew I was on my way to International House. She wondered if I knew how important that job would be and she quizzed me for an hour. I asked if she would come and work with me. So it was done; the most important action I ever took for International House.

Maze seemed a bit surprised, but he himself rather liked dodging the proper way of doing things. So eighteen months later, after travelling again through Asia and India (thanks to one of her professorial admirers) at the age of 61, Rosalie in Hong Kong received the official invitation. Her biographer observed:

All her previous experience with students, refugee intellectuals with problems of accommodation and adjustment, her time in India and travels abroad seemed to fall into a preordained pattern, for under the terms of her appointment she was to be '... resident adviser, guide, philosopher and friend, person around whom the institution moves and who makes it a home instead of an institution — this is the job we want you to do in your own unique way' wrote Graeme.

It was exciting at City Road. Without doubt there would be a House, for there it was just down the road, emerging from the scaffolding. And without doubt there would be enthusiastic residents, for they were already seeking entry. Even before moving over there, a young architecture student had found my office in the Vice-Chancellor's quadrangle. Harry Bergsteiner, still with his German accent, said that he had read about International House and he wanted to be one of our Australian residents. As his young knee was showing clearly through a hole in his jeans, at a time when this was not a fashion statement, it was clear that he was serious when he said he could not afford the fees. (These had been set at $18 per week for full board and lodging. Members of the Board had been disappointed that they were so high, even if lower than those of the colleges, but they accepted that it was necessary, in spite of the University's subsidies.) Harry's expression of interest was noted. We started thinking about bursaries and I had a vision of a life of fund-raising stretching down my working years. Harry went away to get himself a cadetship in the public service, solving his own financial challenge. When he visited City Road it was to fill out our first residence application form. He would proceed to make a wonderful contribution to the life of the House in those formative first years. Twenty-five years later he wrote:

> The reality which evolved from the dream more than measured up to the expectations. I clearly recall my excitement when I first read about International House. This sense of excitement never left me during the three and a bit years which I actually spent in the House. They were extraordinarily enriching years in so many ways.

Professor Elkin liked surveys and helped Professor Don Spearritt survey the graduate student population on campus. We concluded that it might not be easy to balance our planned 'quotas'. What delight we felt when Margot Austin (now Dr Honeyman, Senior Research Scientist at the Walter and Eliza Hall Institute for Medical Research in Melbourne) and Diana Evans (now Professor Anderson at the University of Bradford in the UK), two women science postgraduates, one Australian and one from Wales, walked in at City Road and said 'This is for us'.

As was her custom, Rosalie talked at length among her large circle of friends about what she was up to. Mostly good support came from this; but also one last little flurry of collegiate opposition. The retired Master of Wesley, ironically an old friend, who in his position as Deputy Chancellor had earlier questioned the need for an International House (for wasn't his College with its large population of overseas students all that was needed?), formally approached me one day and expressed much concern that what I was asking of our Deputy Director was beyond her. I was amused. She was furious.

The Provisional Board of Management did not meet after September 1965 until May 1966. They were happy then to learn that the building was on target for completion in November. They were less delighted to hear that the cost had increased to $752,438; and they received a very long report from the Director on overseas International Houses. He also reported that there was a suggestion that a 'Sydney University International House Women's Committee' be established to raise funds for the House's ongoing needs and to assist in other ways. The Board resolved to ask Kathleen O'Neil, the wife of the Deputy Vice-Chancellor, to convene such a committee.

Kath O'Neil agreed. Why would she not? It was all her idea in the first place, as I discovered when Harold Maze had suggested that my wife and I might like to ask the O'Neils to dinner with them at our house, as they were really interested in International House. A neighbour over our back fence had also told me of Kath O'Neil's interest, and her own. The neighbour was Gwen Robson, an ally of Kath's from their Kindergarten Committee days, who also came to work tirelessly for IH and for overseas students' wives and children. My wife has written elsewhere of our experience of Sydney University dinners. On this occasion inconsequential dinner chatter did not get in the way of the business of the evening. Kath had her team already briefed, her plans of campaign in rough but very ready form and her long-range goals in place. I noticed at the time that there were two immediate priorities. One was that she would not only convene a first meeting but she would continue as the Convenor of that committee. Presidents, secretaries and treasurers would come and go on an annual, elected basis; the Convenor would remain. The second was that Mrs Thelma Bate would be steered to work for the University of New South Wales.

Thelma Bate, the only woman who attended those Appeal Committee meetings in the Vice-Chancellor's rooms (where the quantity of Vice-Chancellorian whisky consumed increased with the difficulties in the Committee's work), was officially the Chair of the Rotary Women's Furnishing Sub-committee. The money raised by that committee does not appear to have been kept separate from the general funds or earmarked for furnishings. There is ample evidence of Thelma Bate's work and of the teams of women who supported her. The wife of a federal politician and a leading force and office-bearer in the Country Women's Association, she was a dynamic, powerful and focussed woman. Two big fund-raising events which gave the appeal a late, much-needed fillip, a weekend car race meeting at Oran Park and a sell-out star-studded preview of the film *Mary Poppins*, were her work in the days when the title 'event manager' had not entered the lexicon. One of the committee's activities that was carried on for a number of years beyond the main appeal was a popular International Children's Film Festival, organised by Mrs Valda Lyle in the Wallace Theatre. Kath O'Neil had been the Chair of the Sydney University Auxiliary of Thelma Bate's committee. The Auxiliary had set out to raise £200 to cover the furnishing of two rooms and, as Kath O'Neil proudly remembered, they had raised £2000.

Thelma Bate and Kath O'Neil had much in common. They were immensely talented, intelligent women who lived their lives in a pre-liberated era, making a career of voluntary work in auxiliary organisations. International House owes a huge debt to both of them and their co-workers. These two just were not intended by the gods to work together.

Kath O'Neil did indeed, in the conventional sense, convene an inaugural meeting of the Sydney University International House Women's Committee. It was held in the anteroom of the Great Hall. Many of the women who attended that first meeting would become known to generations of residents as they continued to serve the House for over twenty years. Una Henderson, who would manage the House library for years, had her children with her. Matthew rolled Smarties down the brown lino floor and offered a few to his sister Penelope, who was in a baby basket. We would see Matthew in the House later when he called in on his way home from school to be coached in history by his aunt, Mollie Burns, when she was resident Assistant Director, after her retirement as Senior Graduate Assistant in the University. That is the same Mollie Burns who had found temporary accommodation for me and my family when we came to Sydney; who had with such care and concern administered the scholarships of many of our international students; who had visited alumni around the world, even when it meant riding pillion on a motor scooter with former IH resident Piyara lal Raina as he tried to avoid the cattle on Mysore's monsoon-flooded roads; who generously helped make the Belanglo cabin possible; who maintained the House garden; and who continues to support the House through the endowment of a valuable scholarship. Her niece, Penelope, the baby in the basket, would become a university student and an IH resident, and followed in the tradition of those volunteering women when she supported the House residents' 'Meals on Wheels' program in the Waterloo slums and who, in the next century, would be working for refugees.

The contributions of Kath O'Neil's Women's Committee in fund-raising, help with English, hospitality and management of the shop in the House will surface from time to time in future chapters. In 1966, valuable as it was, there were already some thorns in the bed of roses. After an early meeting, the wife of one of the college heads came into my office in some agitation. She wondered if I realised that it appeared that some members of the Women's Committee believed that they would be running the House! I was aware that there was scope for quite a bit of discussion and clarification in this area, but I believed that head-on confrontation at this stage might lead to the baby being thrown out with the bath water. That lady shook her head in sorrow and kept thereafter to her own college.

Perhaps I should have realised that not everyone could share my awkward approach. For the excitement and the enthusiasm of the new committee did indeed lead to us losing, almost before she had begun, a staff person who had much to offer the International Student Centre we were trying to create. She would, as Program Director, have been the perfect partner to Rosalie McCutcheon. A struggle ensued, certain 'teeth had to be drawn' I was informed, even within the Women's Committee, and the staff member decided that she would rather work elsewhere.

Her role as Program Director was taken up, in his 'spare time', by Dr Peter Simpson, a brilliant young lecturer in chemistry, who moved into residence. With Dr Michael Rathgeber from the Physics Department, Dr Bill Mulder from anthropology, and Roy Whitecross from the Registrar's office, Peter was one of the people I had sought out during the months when I would lunch in the University Staff Club.

The building was handed over on 8 November 1966. There had been one last flurry of concern involving the architect's particular joy, the main Rotunda Common Room (later to be named the Wool Room). The specified chandelier (which later inspired Trevor Allen's design of the House's beautiful logo) would be expensive but, unlike anything else in the House, had not been replaced by a more modest alternative. The urbane Walter Bunning gently did not hear, and there is a suspicion that his own generosity might have been involved. Money could not resolve the other problem: the concern of some people that the open banisters of the gallery would be immodestly revealing from below, given the mini-skirt fashion of the time. A sober sub-committee formed for the purpose assembled in the room and recorded careful observations while a range of available young women paraded on the gallery. The Tasmanian oak banisters were retained.

As the summer approached and the students thinned out on campus, the dreary logistics began. We took delivery of 130 beds, 360 chairs, 120 table lamps, 500 teaspoons, 360 blankets and on and on down my dog-eared foolscap hand-written lists. Deliveries, of course, had to be dovetailed with fitting carpets and hanging curtains, while our suppliers were, in cheerful Australian mid-century custom, proceeding to close up shop for the silly season.

The House would be austerely furnished with essentials. Somehow or other we would raise the money later and the place would look less bare. There was no doubt that every bed would be needed. By the end of October there were already 139 applications for places in 1967.

Anne Seale was busy keeping the applicants' files in order. She had come from the Registrar's office to join Rosalie and me, cheerfully took on all the secretarial work and, with the help of the University Accounts Department, became the House Bursar. (She later became a student in Social Work, resided in the House and married Demetrius Gotsis.) When the time came for us to find Anne's offsider, who would manage the manual plug-and-cord switchboard, sitting welcomingly at the front desk opposite the main entrance, Anne said: 'We must have Pauline Seaich — she is wasted over at the Registrar's Office.' Margaret Telfer, the Registrar, made it difficult for the young Pauline to transfer, but, to the joy of generations of House residents, Pauline Seaich (later Kennedy) stuck to her decision to come over to International House. As residents moved in there were, of course, rumours. One rumour, which we all rather liked — and which was not then regarded as politically incorrect — was that the Director chose his staff on the basis of their looks. This was not true.

Miraculously, it all fell into place, with much help from the University Office of Works, Purchasing and Accounts Offices, and those architects on the Maze corridor — help which would continue for years. There were excited housemaids with brand new vacuum cleaners and shiny buckets and mops. Furniture was allotted according to five different colour schemes through the study bedrooms. As these rooms were all practically identical we thought that no two adjoining ones should be furnished in the same colours! On 11 November, Rosalie McCutcheon moved into the small flat on level 1 and four postgraduate men from Wesley College shifted their belongings over and took up rooms scattered through the House to guard it. Karl Wehrhahn was one of them. He subsequently returned as a resident and, as I write, is still often seen in the House with Tjhioe Lan Tan, his wife of nearly forty years, who was also one of the early House residents. The House was ready to promote friendship and understanding — and romances.

Contracts having been signed with Nationwide Food Services and also for linen hire and laundry, our first real residents and transient guests moved in on 9 January 1967. It was about this time that every lock in the building had to be changed due to malfunctioning of the elaborate 'maison keying' system.

On the first Friday of the first term, when the House was full, every seat in the dining room was occupied when we held our version of the IH Sunday Supper. The cafeteria was transformed in the soft light. Elegant and colourful national costumes and jewellery had chased scruffy student garb into oblivion. There were flowers and there was music. The 126 residents had come from Japan, England, Malaysia, Singapore, Thailand, Hong Kong, India, Pakistan, Korea, Indonesia, Fiji, the USA, Uruguay, Canada, Egypt, Burma, Iran, Wales and Australia. Forty-one of them were Australian men, forty-six were overseas men; there were twenty Australian women and nineteen women from overseas. Five were academic staff of the University and one was an Assistant Registrar. (There were at the time about 650 overseas students on campus, the category being defined as an enrolled student who held a foreign passport with an Australian student visa.) The guest room was occupied by two visiting Russian physicists. There were 60 non-resident members enrolled: twenty-one Australian men (including some senior University staff) and nineteen Australian women, with four overseas women and sixteen overseas men.

There had been misgivings about whether the traditional Candlelight Ceremony would fit into the Australian scene, but we decided to try, modifying the pattern only by having the pledge taken in each resident's first language: 'As light begets light, so love, friendship and goodwill are passed from one to another. We who have come from many nations to live in one fellowship in International House promise one another to pass the light wherever we go.' It was an emotional experience for many people. We were struck by the fact that in the recitation of 27 pledges, English was used only three times. While one knew that many of the residents were daily operating with the handicap of using a foreign tongue, suddenly that academic knowledge became real. That would be how International House would 'work'. We were up and going.

The International House Members' Association was formed, with Michael Hwang as its first Chairperson. Michael was a law graduate from Oxford, doing postgraduate work in Sydney before returning to practise in Singapore. There is no need to explain the 'I' or the 'H' in IHMA. But why not an 'S' for students, or an 'R' for residents? Because every resident, whether undergraduate or senior University staffer, would belong to this one organisation and because it was hoped that non-resident members would be fully involved.

Officially the House would not be open until 16 June at 3 pm. Planning the ceremony caused some angst among the Rotarian representatives. As Rotary's job was completed and as the University's ownership came into effect, there were inevitable disappointments and tensions. Trivial as it might have been compared with the project they had brought to fruition, the fact that it represented a triumphal conclusion seemed to weigh more with the Rotarians than that it signalled a wonderfully exciting commencement. It was agreed that the Chancellor, Sir Charles McDonald, should preside and the Governor of New South Wales, Sir Roden Cutler VC, should be given the honour of declaring the building open; precedence for seating on the dais was settled; and incongruous elegant furnishings came over from the Vice-Chancellor's suite. The day dawned black and heavy. The Sydney rain bucketed down — as it used to do in that era and as it did over the next twenty years whenever IH opened a new wing or invited large numbers of guests to the House.

The second level of the Rotunda was crowded with wet but happy guests. Those who had laboured long had their moment of public acknowledgement. Howard Cook, President of the New York International House, and Sheridan Warrick, Director of the Berkeley House, were there in enthusiastic support and encouragement — and stayed to do likewise at the following Candlelight Dinner and the great ball. The Vice-Regal salute rang out from the primitive borrowed tape recorder, and the Governor's apposite speech surprised me. I had learned much from Harold Maze and much about him — and I was still learning, for when I commented on the speech, the Irish brogue was strong as he said: 'Oh yes. I scribbled a few notes which I thought might be helpful and all and dropped them down to Government House. They are busy people and all you know.'

Afternoon tea in the dining room followed the formal ceremony. There had been some manoeuvring as to who would accompany the Vice-Regal party downstairs and where others might place themselves to ensure a polite bow or curtsy. A result of Walter Bunning's bridge link between the Rotunda and the first dormitory wing and our mistake in not bringing the Rotunda stairs down to the cafeteria level, was that congestion was a problem then, as ever since, on big occasions. Three hundred people had to move across from the Rotunda to the residence, down the stairs and back through the corridor to the dining room.

As the Governor had an artificial leg, I had arranged that the lift in the residence wing would be held at level 2 so that the Vice-Chancellor, Justice McLelland and I, while the assembly stood in the Wool Room, could take him down one floor and escort him through the narrow corridor ahead of the crowd. The lift was there, waiting for us. The doors closed. Instead of descending, the car rose. It stopped at level 3, the doors opened and a throng of people (where had they come from?) were shooed away. Frantic pushing of buttons had no effect. Relentlessly we were taken up to level 4, waited for the doors to open… and so on. All the way up to level 8; and then the performance was repeated all the way down to level 1. An ordinary mortal might have seen that there was something to smile at in all of this. Sir Roden was a great man, but on this, as on a later occasion at IH, he showed that if he had a sense of humour he did not let it interfere with the dignity of the office. Nor did he find it amusing when, on reaching level 1, the lift doors opened

Opening Ceremony, 16 June 1967: His Excellency Sir Roden Cutler VC, Governor of NSW (5th from l), being welcomed by Sir Charles McDonald, Chancellor of the University of Sydney

to reveal a tight pack of excited humanity blocking his passage to thc dining room. Sir Roden's height, walking stick, dignity and rugby past achieved what I could not. Eventually he made his way to the cold tea and the vanished refreshments, graciously acknowledging the deep curtsy that Mrs Bate had waited patiently to present. As I farewelled him later at the front steps, there was just a trace of a grin as he said: 'I wish you well. This is going to be a great place.'

Sources

University of Sydney Archives:
  International Houses Appeal Committee, Minutes and Correspondence
  Sydney University International House Provisional Board of Management, Minutes
  University of Sydney Senate, Minutes
  Students Representative Council, Minutes and Correspondence
  IH Council Minutes

IH Archives:
  Oral histories recorded by Dr Christiana Campbell: W. H. Maze, A. P. Elkin, Geoff Howe, Sleath Lowrey, Ian Hudson, Doreen Langley, Pauline Seaich Kennedy, Rosalie McCutcheon, Kathleen O'Neil, Sir Harold Wyndham, Graeme de Graaff.
  Dr Campbell's notes of her own research, attached to these interviews. (Christiana Campbell was an American alumna of the Chicago International House. It was there as a postgraduate student that she met her Australian husband. Keith Campbell became professor of Agricultural Economics in the University of Sydney, while Christiana was a senior lecturer in History. On her retirement she became President of the Women's Committee, and devoted much time to assembling this oral history. The Campbells' daughter was a resident in the House.)

Rotary Club of Sydney Archives

de Graaff Archive:
  'Excerpts from the Memoirs of Harry Edmonds', 4th edition, 1983
  Pauline Seaich Kennedy's Presentation Album

Publications:
  June Epstein, *Rosalie McCutcheon: a memoir* (Henley Beach, SA: Rosalie McCutcheon Memorial, 1998)
  Paul Henningham, *Seventy-Five years of Service: Rotary in Australia, Papua New Guinea and the Solomon Islands 1921–1996* (Parramatta: Rotary Down Under, 1996)
  Ross Humphreys, *Of Many Nations: A History of International House, the University of Melbourne* (Parkville, Vic.: International House, University of Melbourne, 2004)
  Alex Mitchell, *District 975 of Rotary International of Rotary International 1927–1983* (Sydney: District 975 of Rotary International, 1984)

Chapter Two

1967 to 1969

John Gascoigne

In the three critical years from 1967 to 1969, International House, Sydney University, largely took shape as a community. The foundational buildings — the Rotunda and the eight-storey residential block — had been erected by the time of the opening of the House in 1967, but it was in those first years that much of the institutional DNA of IH was laid down. In that early period, then, the raw buildings began to be transformed into a living community with its own ways of doing things that made IH a distinctive place to live.

Many people helped to create that early but enduring IH spirit, though two stood out particularly: the Director, Graeme de Graaff and the Deputy Director, Rosalie McCutcheon. Although they presided over a residence that was different in many ways from the traditional church-affiliated colleges, interestingly enough, both had strong roots in more traditional forms of university life. For five years during his years as an honours BA and as an MA student at the University of Melbourne, Graeme de Graaff lived in at Queen's, a Methodist college, retaining sufficiently warm memories of it to accept the post of Vice-Master on his return from his postgraduate studies in philosophy at Oxford. At Oxford, too, Graeme de Graaff experienced another form of traditional college life at Balliol College which, for all the outdated regulations about students being locked up by a particular hour, he saw as providing quite a vibrant community of scholars — even though more could have been done to help overseas students. The imprint of these years was evident one night when, called upon to offer a traditional grace at a

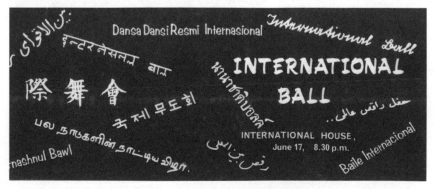

Ticket for the first IH Ball, 1967

House dinner to mark his birthday, he reeled off without hesitation a Latin grace.

Though he had been nurtured in more traditional institutions, it was nonetheless Graeme de Graaff's goal to remould the pattern of student residences into a new shape which would better meet the needs of overseas students — whose problems had been brought home to him both at Melbourne and Oxford. Even as a schoolboy at an Anglican school with links with Africa, some sense of the difficulties of foreign students had been awakened in him. As he put it in a graduation address of 1967 (reprinted in the *Union Recorder*, 15 June 1967), the goal now was to further develop the forms of a college that, at the University of Sydney, went back to the establishment of St Paul's in 1857, and to produce a new type of institution. One of its chief purposes would be 'to physically express the fact that this University is glad that the foreigner has come'.

In different ways, too, Mrs McCutcheon, a graduate of Adelaide, was very much at home in the world to which the existing colleges had largely catered. She could preside over a tea party with all the grace and charm of a hostess, but combined with this a real concern for those who might feel left out or ill at ease in such largely Anglo-Saxon rituals. In her own way she still retained something of the world of genteel living in the relaxed atmosphere of IH: she made a point of 'dressing for dinner'

Mrs Rosemary Berrick, volunteer archivist, and
Mrs Rosalie McCutcheon, first Deputy Director, 1973

even though this might simply mean changing one informal outfit for another. Whatever she did was animated by the religious idealism that had taken her to India with her missionary husband who died there within a year. Much of her career thereafter had been linked with the Student Christian Movement and it was through that body, which sought to combine intellectual reflection on Christianity with practical aid, that she met Graeme de Graaff and found her way to International House. At various times she had lived and worked in Sri Lanka, India, Malaysia and Hong Kong and, as the *Sydney Morning Herald* of 26 December 1966 put it, she came to the House as one who 'had along association with Asia and its people, particularly students'.

As the resident 'philosopher, guide and friend' she did much to translate ideals into action by providing a ready ear for those, whether from home or abroad, who had problems. Sometimes too ready an ear: others worried about the effect on her health of late night tea and sympathy sessions, but Mrs Mac (as she was always known) was not to be deflected from what she saw as her duty. Mrs Mac was one to do good by stealth and, as she herself acknowledged, her job was 'like an iceberg — one-third seen, two-thirds unseen'. Her role did not lend itself easily to a precise job description being 'a sort of catalyst in the house — [to] modify loneliness, to listen — and see beyond present problems; to spark off others into personal interactions'. Originally

Reception: Paul Gottlieb and Pauline Seaich (Kennedy), 1969

there were plans for a resident Dean of Women Students but, in the event, Mrs Mac became Dean of both women and men students and, up to a point, also took on the task of another proposed but not realised IH position, a tutor in English for overseas students.

Mrs Mac formally resigned from the post in June 1972 but for many years thereafter continued to be one of IH's guiding stars, coming back to fill in when needed. At a House dinner in March 1975 she described her 'own years here' as 'among the most enriching years of my life'. IH she saw as 'no ordinary place', in part because it 'is large enough to provide diversity and stimulus but small enough for everyone of you (if you want to!) to know everyone in the House by sight'.

Along with the work of the Director and Deputy-Director, the early IH presented a friendly face to the world, thanks to the early incumbents of the front office: Anne Seale (later Gotsis), who became House Bursar, bringing in her wake from the Registrar's office Pauline Seaich (now Kennedy). Pauline served in various capacities from its beginning until 1984 (and again, after a break, from 1988 until 1993), being in turn receptionist, House secretary and Bursar and, subsequently, Assistant Director with responsibility for the program of activities. She helped to provide IH with a sense of continuity and 'institutional memory' and in her various roles her sunny disposition helped to ward off at least some of the squalls to which any community is prone.

In a university where, hitherto, student residences had been largely linked with the churches, the establishment of International House meant looking for different models on which to draw. An exception to this generalisation was the non-denominational Women's College, which is perhaps part of the reason that its Principal, Doreen Langley, played such an active part in the first decades of the House. As a place intended primarily for mature students from both home and abroad and as an institution that then took the very adventurous step of being co-ed, IH was not likely to mesh readily with many of the sorts of activities that drew the other residential colleges together. Quite accurately, Graeme de Graaff predicted to a Rotary audience back as early as 1966 that IH was not likely 'to field teams in the traditional Australian sports' (though he did hold out some hopes for table tennis and billiards). However, he hoped, 'we will perhaps gain in community pursuits new to the colleges (and out of place in them)'.

It was for this reason that Sam Dimmick, Warden of International House at the University of Melbourne, and de Graaff lost no time after the opening of the Sydney House in organising an International Houses corroboree. Always with an eye to acknowledging the Melbourne collegiate pattern, Dimmick arranged for David Darling to provide the biggest and most expensive silver rose bowl he could find as a perpetual trophy for this event. For the first corroboree, Sydney and Brisbane sent teams down to Melbourne over the Easter vacation. They were lavishly hosted and entertained.

The sporting events — in soccer, table tennis, tennis and darts — might have lacked some of the intensity of the Melbourne or Sydney intercollegiate competitions, but they made up for this in curing a feeling of otherness and exclusion which the Melbourne IH pioneers had been feeling. And the inclusion of a debating contest was a subtle indication that the International Houses were not just pale imitations of the older institutions, but were pointing to an alternative ethos. (The Intercollegiate Debate at Sydney University years later came from the desire of the Director of International House and the Principal of Sancta Sophia to hint that there were different ways of relating to each other.) The best thing about that first corroboree, it was evident, was what it did for the group of people who went to Melbourne from Sydney. A number of individuals from Australia and many other countries came back with a gleam in their corporate eye. 'Understanding' had been advanced in one great leap, a phenomenon which would be noticed over the years whenever a number of residents engaged in a House activity.

IH also differed from the other colleges in that, as a place for overseas students, it needed to be open all year round. An early indication of the way in which such a difference changed the character of the institution was the 1968 Christmas Day dinner for 150 overseas students (which was complemented by a Christmas party for the students from the neighbouring primary school). IH also differed in expecting residents to look after themselves more and it employed fewer domestic staff. In the early days, then, it was cheaper than the colleges (when it opened board and lodging fees were $16–$22 a week). This difference, however, waned with time, in part because IH students were no more enthusiastic about performing domestic chores than other college students.

Though there had been an International House at Melbourne for the previous ten years and one had opened at the University of Queensland in 1966, the main model was the 'mother house' of International Houses in New York, established with Rockefeller largesse in the 1920s, as were the ones in Chicago and Berkeley which followed soon afterwards. From New York came the motto 'That Brotherhood May Prevail' — inscribed in stone over the main door of the 'mother-house' — and a ritual, the Candlelight Ceremony, at the House's closing dinner for the year.

As rituals do, this helped to provide an outward and visible sign of what IH stood for. Holding a candle, some residents recited the pledge to promote international fellowship; the New York-derived

Nuli Lemoh
(President of SUIHAA 2004–2006)
at the first Candlelight Ceremony, 1967

ceremony was given a Sydney twist in that, instead of one individual reciting the pledge, a representative of each country with residents in the House spoke the words in their own language on behalf of their own countrymen and women, concluding with the Australian representative. The atmosphere of the occasion was heightened by the extinguishing of all lights apart from the large candle in the centre of the room and the way in which light was gradually restored as members of each national group relit their candles from this central candle. Those with national dress would wear it, while others donned more formal attire than generally prevailed in the informal atmosphere of IH. In the early days some capped the night off with a trip to Luna Park. IH residents repaired to that amusement park en masse in 1969 thanks to the generosity of the park's general manager, the Rotarian Ted Hopkins, who allowed them entry gratis.

For International House, Sydney, it was the Berkeley model that loomed particularly large since it, too, was closely linked with one particular university, in contrast to the New York one which catered to the city at large with its many educational institutions. But at Berkeley, as at New York, there was a strong sense that the mission of the House was to reach beyond the residents to overseas students more generally and this formed part of the founding philosophy of IH. The institution, as Graeme de Graaff put it in his graduation address of 1967, was 'a combination of a residence and a non-residential International Centre'. One of the more painful lessons of IH's history has been that this particular aspect of the foundation houses in the USA could not be readily transplanted.

The focus in the early years was naturally on building up IH's own internal identity, but right from the beginning the idea of combining a hall of residence with an international centre was present. By 1969 this outreach function of IH was being given stronger prominence. In that year Stephen Clark and then Lesley Cohen were appointed successively as full-time Program Directors with the aim of fostering not only a program of activities within the House but also of attracting overseas students to participate, even though they might not be House residents. As Stephen Clark told the *Sydney Morning Herald* (13 February 1969): 'My main function will be to widen the role of the house into a real international centre.' The hope was that, in doing this, Australians and overseas students would move 'out of their little insular groups' — and, indeed, that the House's outreach might go beyond students to 'national groups within the community'.

Any such widening of IH's role had to build on its existing program of activities. IH's first report in 1969 underlined the importance of such a program in creating the house's identity: 'The distinctive thing about any IH, which distinguishes it from an ordinary hall of residence, is the program of activities designed to bring overseas and Australian students into meaningful contact with each other.' In the House's early years, there were special events which highlighted particular cultures, as when the Laotian students welcomed Prince Souvanna Phouma, the Prime Minister of Laos.

From IH's beginnings, an International Night with performances representing different cultures became a major annual event. This distinctive and enduring feature of IH life grew out of the House Dinners which were held at the beginning and end of each of three terms (in contrast to what was then the general practice in the colleges of having formal dinners every night). At such House Dinners, instead of the usual informal cafeteria meal, the tables were set and had tablecloths, there were candles, waiters served the meal, there was live music and a speaker; residents and non-resident members brought guests, often their university supervisors. Many of the overseas students would wear national costumes.

It was this custom which gave Heng Keng Chiam the idea in 1968 of having an International Night. It was to be a parade of national costume with commentary. And that was indeed what began the first International Night (an event which has been held every year since). A fresh-faced Brian Farmer in black tuxedo was MC. (He would later serve many years on the House Council and as its Chair.) The idea had taken fire and the opening parade was followed by a series of presentations of song and dance in which the various national groups did indeed add to the cross-cultural understanding of many residents.

35

Australian residents sometimes found it difficult to decide on what was authentic Australian culture or garb. It was surprising how every few years a new generation would come up with the idea of enacting the *Man from Ironbark*. But even at this early stage some of the presentations were creative rather than authentic. Residents long remembered with joy one contribution from the Papua New Guinea contingent led by Bernard Narokobi (later Attorney-General of his country). Impressed by some of the group's detailed expositions of the meaning of the dances they were about to perform, Bernard delivered a lengthy account of the song and dance he and his fellows (standing behind him shivering in their feathered costumes) would present. The audience tried hard to follow, but were relieved when Bernard gave every sign of lifting his copper home-made 'flute' to a playing position, thus signifying the end of the talk and the beginning of the culture. But he lowered the flute to deliver one last sentence: we could forget all he had just said, because he had made it all up. Papua New Guinea, we would understand, was made up of many disparate cultural groups. While he and his fellow performers were indeed good mates, they had been lumped together by IH as 'Papua New Guinea'. The only common language they had was English, nor did they have a folk story or song between them. It was a great dance.

One of the great attractions of International Night was the multicultural cuisine which accompanied it — especially since in those days ethnic restaurants were not as ubiquitous as they were to become. In later years both the number of acts from different lands and the number of dishes at International Night grew to the point when there had to be separate nights for the performances and the culinary extravaganza. The need for the spirit of the House to be reflected in that central part of community life — the food — took some time to be realised. When prominent members of the IH community reviewed the early years of the House in 1972, one of the comments made was, 'Overseas students find the food disagreeable'. Slowly, both in the House and in the wider community, Australia's traditional limited culinary repertoire began to catch up with a wider world.

In the meanwhile, overseas students could use the floor kitchens to cook the food with which they were familiar — an important part of maintaining their own identity and alleviating homesickness. Such was the theme of an article in the *Sun Herald* (18 June 1967), headed 'A little bit of home', describing how Asian students (both male and female) at IH kept their culinary traditions alive, even if it meant importing some spices from home. For some students, Anglo-Saxon eating habits took some getting used to: for Asians mixing sweet and savoury foods seemed strange and the breakfast cereals seemed 'tasteless'. It was easy, too, for Australians to take for granted the use of cutlery, at least until they tried using chopsticks.

Meals were at the heart of the endeavour to make IH a real community and to establish living traditions within the House. Even the choice of furniture was important in helping to establish ways in which residents could interact. One of the early inspired decisions was the choice of round tables which encouraged people to converse with a larger group. The importance of conversation was underlined by the instruction given to the kitchen staff to leave a table uncleared overnight rather than break up an animated conversation. Other mealtime conventions were established early: members of staff did not sit at the same table and when someone got up to get tea or coffee, it was the done thing to ask all those at the table if they would like some. Meals were also an occasion to display the absence of rules. There was no high table and no dress rules. The whole emphasis of the House was on treating residents as mature students who could make their own decisions. Somewhat to Mrs Mac's dismay, this extended as far as allowing residents to come to meals barefoot.

With food comes wine (though that was not as true then as now). One of the early ventures at IH was the foundation of a wine cellar. At the initiative of Brian Farmer, contacts were made with various wine suppliers and, more importantly, with the Licensing Sergeant at Redfern Police Station. Given that Sydney's licensing laws at the time were pretty strict, it was anticipated that there would be all sorts of problems; however, since wine cellars existed in some of the colleges, it was expected that there would be a way through the morass of regulation and legal constraints.

The Licensing Sergeant was very clear (and of great assistance) and laid down two basic principles: money could not change hands (that is, customers could not buy anything for cash) and the wine cellar could not and should not make a profit. The first problem was easily solved by asking residents to establish credit in their name by subscribing a set amount and the second by selling wine and beer to residents at cost price with a very small mark-up to cover administrative costs. But, alas, a small profit did ensue and the only solution was to throw a party to dispose of it — creative accounting at its most inventive! In contrast to most student residences there were no regulations about the use of alcohol since, happily, there was no need for them.

One of the most valuable traditions (or non-traditions) of IH was the absence of a 'grog culture'. This owes much to the large number of postgraduate students and of Asian students who were not greatly attracted to the doubtful blandishments of Australian pubs. The early foundation of the wine cellar did, however, do much to establish the connection (which is taken for granted in much of Europe) between wine and food and, with it, conversation — thus acting as a brake on binge drinking, the doleful effects of which were readily to be seen around the campus (and, in particular, in some of the colleges).

The lack of any elaborate regulations about the use of alcohol was an instance of IH's laissez-faire approach to rules more generally. For one of the things that set IH apart from the colleges was the insistence that it was a place for adults and that therefore rules should be kept to a minimum. In its early days IH did indeed draw on an older constituency than was later to be the case (in 1969 the average age of residents was 26). One of the intentions in establishing IH was to provide a home for postgraduates and when it first opened some forty per cent of residents were postgraduates (though this was to decline as the years went by). Disproportionately, postgraduate residents tended to be from overseas and undergraduates from Australia.

The Director's hope that this maturity in residents would translate into a willingness by them to undertake some of the running of the House when it came to matters like discipline was not fully realised. One of the early formative experiences was establishing the limits to what residents were prepared to do and the line between the activities of the IH administration and the resident body, the International House Members' Association (IHMA). Not surprisingly, students who came from abroad and were used to very different ways of doing things were not anxious to sit in judgement over fellow residents. From very early on, however, IHMA was to play a key role in fostering social activities within the House and it soon became (and remained) a core part of the life of the House. One of the main tasks of the House in 1967 was the establishment of the IHMA and its constitution. In the first two years its activities were both encouraged and facilitated by the then part-time resident Assistant Director (Program), Dr Peter Simpson, a lecturer in Chemistry.

Few of his students will have forgotten Peter Simpson. Rather coyly the *Union Recorder* (15 June 1967) referred to his lectures as being 'not only erudite and clear, but reputed to have other qualities too'. For his students expected not only to be instructed but also to be entertained: at a certain point in the lecture the cry went up, 'Joke, joke', and students were rarely disappointed. This ebullience carried over to his activities in International House where, as a resident member of staff, he did much to mould its early traditions.

It was Peter Simpson who represented the House in March 1968 at an Orientation Week symposium on 'Colleges: Mainstreams of a University or Academic Backwaters?' organised by the Women's Union (for there was then a female and a male union, a reminder of how daring IH was in accommodating women and men under the one roof). The report of proceedings in the *Union Recorder* (7 March 1968) was a little tongue-in-cheek in characterising the infant IH as a place where, 'we were led to believe, asexuality and ideals of brotherhood between mature cosmopolitan inmates supposedly provide a lesson to us all'. Peter Simpson was, however, successful in persuading his audience that some of the ideals for which IH stood had been realised and that 'there would be no more wars if Arabs and Jews lived together in the Middle East as well as they did at International House'.

The reference to the Middle East had a very real resonance since, indeed, IH had had to live through the tensions generated by the 1967 Six Day War. One result had been fiery words between Paul Gottlieb, who had immediately volunteered for service in Israel, and Samy Abed from Egypt, but fellowship (if not agreement) had prevailed. A sign that IH was achieving its goals was that when Paul left for Israel, Samy was among those at the airport who saw him off. It is heartening that such traditions continued: in a SUIHAA Newsletter nearly thirty years later, an Israeli alumna observed that her time at IH 'allowed me to see other sides of Islam and of the Arab nation; it gave me a greater hope for peace'.

The *Union Recorder*'s report on this same debate also made a more oblique reference to IH as a place where 'sexual frustrations could be eased by having a seminar on the subject'. Indeed, the IH Newsletter of the previous year reported the proceedings of a seminar on the subject 'Freedom of Sex', attended by '35 enthusiastic listeners, most of whom were males'. It was obviously long remembered, since, in its sober fashion, the House's report for 1969 mentioned that 'a one-day symposium on sex was serious and valuable'. The report then went on to mention that 'the National Union of Australian University Students held its symposium on Vietnam in the House, and the University held a staff–student symposium'. Both items were, in their different ways, a reminder that the House's origins were intertwined with the concerns of the sixties and the youth revolt that accompanied it. As a young institution with its traditions still in formation, however, IH was able to avoid too heated a confrontation between generations.

From its first days, the House had early to learn to cope with minor disappointments and major tragedy. The death while playing squash of Jone Tabaiwalu, the IHMA Chair, in the House's second term was simply shattering. A chief in Fiji and destined, many thought, for leadership at home in the law or politics or both, he was a quiet, forceful presence in both the House and the local Fijian community. It was an event which the House — a deliberately non-religious community — had not worked out how to handle. The Director drank kava with Jone's grieving countrymen and women in a nearby suburb. The House in the end formalised its own grieving with a service in the Chapel of Wesley College, where Jone had lived before deciding that he had an obligation to contribute to the new venture over on City Road. At this Methodist college the tradition of hymn singing appropriately reflected Jone's own background.

When, two years later, Dr Michael Rathgeber died suddenly while attending a conference in Japan, a slightly matured House seemed better able to cope with the distress and sorrow. A large group of residents could meet in a silence which only a Quaker Meeting could emulate and then Michael's family held a memorial service — in the Wool Room at the House.

Within these few short years, from 1967 to 1969, IH had emerged from rather raw beginnings to become a fully-functioning institution with its own distinctive ways of doing things and a busy communal life for the 120 residents who occupied the building by 1969. When it opened, some of the infrastructure still needed a good deal of sorting out: the lift regularly malfunctioned and the fire alarm had a mind of its own. The Director once suffered the indignity of being stuck in the lift while the fire alarm shrieked what turned out to be a quite false alarm — thus allowing lonely contemplation of possible extinction by two different methods. Bare walls and floors only gradually were covered by furnishings and the locks had to be replaced.

The Women's Committee was at its strongest and most active in this period. It continued to invent new ways of raising money and replaying the established methods. The persuasive charm of its Convenor secured from the Australian Wool Board the contribution of carpets, chairs and curtains in the Rotunda, together with a work of art in wool, celebrating the naming of the room as the Wool Room. This wall hanging puzzled several generations of residents until, one summer vacation, moths ravaged it beyond repair.

The wish of this committee to be seen not simply as a source of money was fulfilled, and this partly by very clever ways of presenting events which furthered the aims of the House at the same time as bringing in donations. The Festival of the Four Winds transformed the Wool Room and the cafeteria for a weekend into an international bazaar. A Japanese Night brought the wider community into the presence of dignitaries from the Embassy and to meet some of the future leaders in the House community. The Women's Committee's co-operation with the residents in inviting local schoolchildren to IH hopefully did a little to offset the feeling in the neighbourhood that the University was squeezing them out of their suburb.

The endeavours of the volunteers of this committee did something to clothe the still often-naked structure but, inevitably, the building took some time to be humanised. No doubt a certain amount of 'roughing it' helped to promote an *esprit de corps* and with it a sense that residents were engaged in something special — as indeed they were. For the 'originals' of 1967–1969 built on the often all-too-evident foundations of bricks and mortar much of the human superstructure which made IH a distinctive community.

Sources

This chapter has greatly benefited from the reminiscences of both Graeme de Graaff and Brian Farmer. Otherwise it has been based on the invaluable scrap-books compiled by the former honorary archivist, Rosemary Berrick in the IH archives. These are arranged in chronological order and have been recently catalogued by Jackie Hartley.

IH Archives:

Most relevant to this chapter has been File 1.1 (which covers the years 1957 to 1975) and 1.4 for Rosalie McCutcheon's talk at the dinner on 20 October 1983. Also useful was 1.20 (International House Reports and Reviews), which includes the report on the Seminar 'Review of the Past 5 Years' (20 February 1972).

Chapter Three
The 1970s
John Gascoigne

If it was in the period 1967–70 that the culture of International House began to take shape, it was during the 1970s that IH strengthened and consolidated its sense of what it was and what made it special. By 1970, some of the familiar features that set it apart from the existing colleges were evident. An article in the university student paper, *Honi Soit* (26 January 1970), by the then IH program director, Lesley Cohen, remarked on the way 'The place lacks formality and is without elaborate traditions though it has a few in-bred customs'. The community had begun to bubble though, at least in the author's view, the result was sometimes a bit too vigorous with 'hot air finding a few escape holes in the balloon but no-one coming along to put patches over the holes and seeing if it can become functional again'.

As the seventies progressed, IH came to assume a clearer identity which, in physical terms, was strengthened by the expansion of the House with the erection of the East and Elkin wings. This was also the period when the House was to establish some of the things it was not. Most importantly, the early goal of making it not only a hall of residence but also a centre for overseas students throughout the state was found to be unsustainable — such students felt little identity with an institution in which they did not live, particularly as, in many cases, they did not even attend the University of Sydney. As the decade wore on, too, International House came to resemble other colleges more in being less a residence for postgraduate or older students.

By the House's tenth anniversary in 1977, however, there was a strong sense that it was firmly established and had a special job to do in bringing together overseas and Australian students. It was an occasion, wrote Doreen Langley, that made one 'feel that the House was here to stay, was well established and would go on'. This was underlined by the number of former residents returning to Sydney for the occasion and by the fact, too, that it was celebrated at a dinner in London organised by Nuli and Margaret Lemoh. Among the guests there were myself and my future wife, Kathleen Bock — another of the many IH marriages.

This sense of identity which gave the House its purpose and direction owed much to some key individuals who shaped its character in its early years, including a good deal of the seventies. As the previous chapter has brought out, two that stand out particularly were, of course, the

Emeritus Professor A. P. Elkin,
first Chair of the House and
Finance Committee

Director, Graeme de Graaff, and the Deputy Director, Rosalie McCutcheon. From quite a different perspective, another of IH's early guiding influences was the distinguished anthropologist, Professor A. P. Elkin. Though linked with the embryonic IH as early as 1964, he came to assume a particular importance in its affairs during the 1970s, serving as the Chair of Council from 1972 to 1977 as well as Chair of the House and Finance Committee from 1966 to 1979. Drawing on his wide experience, which included early years as a bank clerk, theological studies which led to his ordination as an Anglican minister and his ground-breaking work in the study of Aboriginal society, he provided a number of clear statements of the philosophy by which IH should be guided. For him, as he wrote in the IH Council's second report in 1972, the House embodied the Greek ideal of an '*Oikumene*', by which he meant 'a community of students from many races, lands, languages, cultures and histories'. Out of such a diverse and variegated meeting of peoples, he hoped, would emerge individuals who could 'glimpse the vision of a community of nations and peoples, which we hope that they will never lose'.

The tenth anniversary was an occasion when Elkin could prompt further reflection on what the House stood for. He formulated the pattern of seminars held to mark the occasion — seminars which were conducted by alumni from the 'Four Geographical, Human, Cultural and Historical "Worlds" of Africa, the Middle East, the Far East and the West'. Something of the thinking behind such a pattern was revealed in his Council's report for 1977. In it he drew an analogy with the way in which all residents bring with them 'a bundle of culture' which, while they are in the House, is enriched by the 'magic' that others bring with them. On leaving, they would go back to their own societies with the same bundle, which is both familiar and yet subtly transmogrified by contact with others: for the aim was not to produce uniformity but, rather, 'variety in unity'.

The House was to play a major part in Elkin's death as well as his life, since he died just after a Council meeting; a major point of debate at that meeting had been whether to employ professional fund-raisers, something he opposed — the notes from the meeting he left behind testify that his intellectual and political faculties were well-honed to the end. Fittingly the South Wing, as it was to be, was renamed the Elkin Wing. At its opening on 13 October 1979, the Governor-General, Zelman Cowen, observed how appropriate it was that among the first to live in the building would be some Aboriginal trainee teacher-aides, thus fulfilling one of Elkin's long cherished goals. Fortunately the Governor-General was unaware that the big day had very nearly been subverted by vandals who covered the foyer walls with graffiti and trailed paint from there to the Elkin Wing — rarely has a carpet been relaid so quickly.

In sustaining the ideals that A. P. Elkin articulated so vividly, the University of Sydney IH benefited from continuing contact with other International Houses. This was particularly important since IH often had only a limited amount in common with the other colleges at the University even though its Director was a member of the organisation of college heads. The very name 'Director' set IH off from the traditional colleges with their Wardens, Masters and the like, as did the fact that there was no residence for the Director within the House. In the early years, too, and for much of the seventies, IH residents were older than those from the colleges and less interested in traditional intercollegiate sports. In 1972 the average age of IH residents was 25 and about half were postgraduate students. This was reflected in the way in which residents were treated as adults. 'Information for Residents' for 1976, for example, struck this note: 'You will notice that this Information Booklet contains few rules and regulations in the normal sense. This is not an oversight. We want this House to be a place where residents may enjoy the greatest degree of freedom possible.' It did hasten to add, however, 'This does not, of course, mean "anything goes"'.

Symbolically IH was located at a considerable distance from the colleges, embodying the shift across City Road into Darlington associated with the expansion of the University in the 1960s. International House was that new-fangled thing, a hall of residence much more directly responsible to the University than a college; in its early days it aroused fears that the University might seek to expand its role in providing student residences to the detriment of the existing colleges. As time wore on, however, some of the differences between IH and other colleges diminished. Residents of the House became younger and IH's reputation for 'no-frills' services became less true as residents sought more creature comforts. Meanwhile, the colleges had to trim their budgets, so they curtailed some of the more labour-intensive services; thus they and IH came more and more to converge in what they offered students. Contact with the colleges was maintained by the Director attending the meetings of heads of colleges and by some spasmodic (and not very glorious) involvement by IH during the 1970s in inter-college soccer. Unfortunately, there was no inter-college competition in table tennis, which was a game avidly pursued in the House.

For much of the seventies, however, the House's sense of being 'special' and embodying a particular philosophy was strengthened by contact with other Australian IHs. There was some contact in the form of debates and the like with the sister institution at the University of New South Wales which had been founded as part of the same largely Rotary-inspired and funded venture as IH at the University of Sydney — though not as much as one might have thought. As described in the previous chapter, the tradition of the corroborees which brought together residents from Houses in Melbourne, Wollongong, Sydney and Brisbane helped to sustain a more generalised IH identity. I vividly recall the bonding experience of going by overnight train with other residents up to Brisbane for one such in 1970. Brisbane was again host in 1974 (when the Sydney IH delegation was dispatched in two cars), while Melbourne did the honours in 1976. Another was also held in Brisbane in August 1978 and the IHMA Newsletter urged residents to rally to the 'mission: To return the IH Trophies for being the top IH' and referred to the destination as 'the land of the peanut and sunshine'. Less competitively, it later acknowledged how 'terrific' was 'the friendship of the Brisbane IH people'.

At a different level, contact between the directors of International Houses around the world, particularly with those at Berkeley and New York, helped to keep the IH flame burning and its sense of its purpose strong. Appropriately, among the guests of honour at the celebrations to mark the tenth anniversary was the Director of IH New York. When the role of the Sydney IH's student centre was being evaluated, it was to Berkeley IH that the Sydney House turned. Irene Prescott, formerly the Director of Community Programs at Berkeley, came and lived in during February and March 1972. She produced a candid report, complimenting Sydney University IH on its role as a residence and its warm and friendly character but questioning the extent to which combining this with a larger outreach role could be realised. One of the reasons for the good relations among residents was IH's relatively small size but, she pointed out, this limited the range of activities that could be offered. In any case, the attempt to cater to the needs of both residents and outsiders had to be thought through more, especially as the existing program tried to do too much and suffered from poor attendances.

Sadly, despite work by many within International House, and particularly by Program Directors such as Belinda Dawson (later Lamb), the role of IH as a centre for overseas students did not take hold. The idea that the House and its facilities could ease their transition to a different culture seemed a fine one and made economic sense, since IH was a going concern which could provide meals and meeting spaces.

Although originally IH's outreach function was intended simply to encompass the University of Sydney, the federal government was prepared to invest in an expanded role whereby IH would become a centre for overseas students throughout New South Wales. The government was becoming more conscious of the need to cater to foreign students who could act as ambassadors for Australia after graduation and so the Minister for Foreign Affairs, William McMahon, opened the International Students' Centre with some fanfare on 12 February 1971. Along with IH's established facilities, it served as a base for the Host Family Scheme which provided contact between overseas students and Australian families and also offered advice on immigration and related matters as well as English conversation classes.

Though it was calculated that there were some five thousand overseas students in New South Wales at universities, technical colleges, hospitals and schools, there were few who were prepared to cross City Road from the main campus, let alone catch the bus from other campuses. I can recall in 1972 the woman in the coffee shop, whose job it was to serve such students, glad to see at least the occasional resident seeking late-night refreshment as a relief from her lonely task. IH did provide a meeting space for officers of the various overseas clubs to get together and, of course, the Wool Room was a good venue for dances and concerts.

Among the residents, however, there was less than whole-hearted enthusiasm for large numbers of non-residents attending functions not directly connected with the IHMA, particularly as this meant instituting more stringent security procedures. One of the final sticking points between IH and the Department of Foreign Affairs which brought to an end the grant and, with it, the Overseas Centre, was a request for the Centre to be able to operate for more extended hours and so it closed on 21 December 1973.

Though the Centre closed, the non-resident program for members of the university continued — albeit with mixed fortunes. It had been a feature of the House from its beginning, again reflecting the underlying philosophy that IH should be more than a residence and should provide a base for international fellowship that went beyond the immediate residents: in 1969, within two years of IH's opening, there were 120 non-resident members. For some, including myself, it was a way of introducing students to IH that led to their becoming residents. There was, however, criticism that some became non-residents for the sake of cheap meals and made little attempt to get to know the residents. The program waxed and waned over the years. As Program Director, Roger Wescombe sought in 1975 to invigorate the scheme, writing that he hoped 'that 1975 will, among other things, be the year of the Non-Resident Member'. The scheme later went into hibernation, but was revived again for a limited number of students in 1985.

Whether resident or non-resident, all members of IH belonged to the IHMA, the main body for organising the activities within the House. It had, by the standards of the time, a considerable budget at its disposal. In 1976 its bulletin announced that it had 'an annual budget of around $1000 with which to promote a wide range of functions as well as to buy newspapers, sports equipment and other utilities'. The Chair of IHMA played an important part in the life of the House, generally meeting with the Director once a week and sitting on the House Council. Under its aegis, and with the assistance of the various Program Directors, the House developed a steady cycle of functions that was consolidated during the 1970s.

The early practice of holding an International Night became institutionalised in this period. In 1975, for example, the program included such diverse offerings as a Thai dance, a Ugandan song, a Hong Kong choir, a Polish dance, Irish songs, a Sri Lankan dance, Indonesian songs, a Japanese tea ceremony and a Malaysian wedding ceremony, followed by 'Food from around the World'. Another annual fixture was the ball — in 1975 held on 1 November and hence called the Hallowe'en Ball. The communal cellar continued to be well patronised and a film club was established.

In some years there was a program of lectures and discussions linked to the theme of international relations and cross-cultural understanding. While Roger Wescombe was Program Director in 1975 (during which time he filled in for Graeme de Graaff for several months while he was ill), there was an interesting series on the great religions of the world, along with nights devoted to particular national cultures, with an Indian and a China night and an evening of Papuan New Guinean films and food. In the following year the Program Director was Michael Bennett who, like Roger Wescombe, a high school teacher, also had a 'day job' (as a lecturer in medieval history). He organised (and contributed to) a successful series of Tuesday night discussions, entitled 'Looking at the Modern World'.

More informal social life within IH was largely based on the floors. 'We shape our buildings', Churchill once wrote of the House of Commons, 'but they also shape us'. One of the most important features of a college or hall is to provide a small community with which one can identify, whether, as in some colleges, it be a staircase or a cluster of rooms (as was to apply in the East Wing and Elkin Wing). In the main multi-storied residence, floors provided the distinctive social groupings. When, in 1975, Erica Sparks (who later served as a resident Assistant Director) suggested ways of welcoming new residents, one was that 'One person on each floor will be responsible for organising the floor "welcoming"; he/she will have some brochures describing the house and its facilities as well as maps etc'. Floors even took on the character of their most high-profile residents: in my day the fourth floor was known as being rather macho.

One source of friction was the phones: with one phone per floor and no system of rostering it fell to those nearest or most civic-minded to answer the phone (perhaps in the hope that the call was for them), go to the room of the resident in question and, as often as not, have to respond to an unanswered knock by returning to the phone to take a message and then return once more to pin it to the said door. This was particularly galling when the message was for one of the many people who made it plain that they consistently adopted a non-involvement policy when it came to answering phones. But such frictions could be oiled and good relations (generally) restored by the many floor parties.

Floors were so much the natural social unit that they were represented within IHMA. In 1976, for example, the IHMA committee consisted of representatives from each of the eight floors (that is, from the seven floors and the East Wing) along with five general representatives elected from the House as whole. Part of the reason so much socialising took place at floor level is that, sadly, the Wool Room, splendid as it was, was too large and not sufficiently homely to attract many residents, although they were drawn to the games and television rooms in the Rotunda above it. The nearby library held many books kindly donated by the Women's Committee and Rotary, but these were rarely consulted; it was more a place for study and escape from a noisy floor or possibly, for the few in twin rooms, one's room-mate.

A perennial item of discussion for IHMA and residents more generally was the food. The comments book in the dining room always made good copy. The IHMA magazine, *Staying Alive,* in 1978 printed some choicer items: 'I've trodden in better', 'I don't know what you are all whingeing about. What do you want for $50 a week — something edible??!!', 'Keep it up, David, Keep it down, Charlie', 'The Hungarian Ghoul-Hash tasted as if it was made from whole, fresh Hungarian Ghouls'. But there were also compliments of a sort: 'I think the food here is pretty good. Anna', followed by 'I think Anna is pretty good'. If one's hunger had not been quelled by the IH meals, the most common resort was to whip up something in the floor kitchen, which left that particular aromatic odour which seemed a part of IH.

Another alternative was to venture into the wider culinary world. This had been going on for some time and the same 1978 bulletin announced the 'IH Supper Club', which 'conducts excursions approximately twice a week in search of food for the mutual enjoyment of its members. Usually 10.30–11.30'. Common resorts were the seedier establishments in Dixon Street, maintained, so it was said, to provide refreshments for the gamblers, who were out of sight. One needed a Chinese interpreter, since the menu consisted of a row of cards in Chinese strung up near the entrance. With a certain nostalgia, the September 1972 SUIHAA Newsletter had announced the demise of one such establishment: 'We regret to announce the closure of the "Fook Lee" eating place in Dixon Street, Sydney, and the threatened death by "tourisation" of the street itself.'

Nineteen seventy-seven saw the unlamented departure of Nationwide, the caterers with whom IH had dealt since its beginning. The Sydney University Union was called in to take its place, though the transition was not smooth. The new catering manager reported in June that there had been 'some traumatic moments during our take-over. Nationwide had been rather unco-operative and we were unable to do much practical work'. Needless to say, as the excerpts above from 1978 indicate, grumbling about the food remained one of the most important bonding experiences among residents. Old hands, however, detected an improvement: Trish Gibson, a resident in 1972, noted in the SUIHAA magazine for 1980 that she had stayed in the House briefly and thought that the food was 100 per cent better.

One issue of concern for the IHMA committee was whether overseas students were sufficiently represented on it. For many such residents, taking time out from their studies to attend meetings held in a foreign language and with unfamiliar conventions was difficult indeed. In 1972

The Cafeteria:
Varavudh Sithipitaks, Amornrat Kovitya, Peter Donkor, 1977

there was a review in the association's structure which resulted in a new type of committee, with overseas students from the different floors being guaranteed a minimum representation. Sunday suppers also increasingly made a point of including international menus. Two years later there was a move for a more thorough-going upheaval in the way the House was conducted, to give more emphasis to its international character, and various manifestos were circulated by both advocates and opponents of change. In the event, a number of the reform leaders left the House in frustration, but the overall result was to refocus IH's attention on its primary goals.

The House was founded with the aim of overseas students meeting Australians and gaining 'a deeper understanding of Australia' and, reciprocally, of giving 'Australian students the opportunity to broaden their outlook through friendship with students from different cultures and backgrounds'. Inevitably, the House's success in achieving these worthy goals was variable. Some groups (including, on occasions, Australians) retreated into national 'ghettos' and dined together, or concocted ethnic meals on the floor kitchens. But, of course, what could appear to Australians to be an 'Asian' table could well be one at which different nationalities from that wide and diverse continent were mixing together — and might even include a number of Australian citizens of Asian background. Michael Bennett recalls one resident from Thailand saying how much it had meant to her to make friends with other young women from Malaysia, Hong Kong and the Philippines.

There was some continuing unease that Australians and overseas students (especially from Asia) did not interact quite as much as would have accorded with the goals of IH. At the 1972 seminar on IH there were comments such as 'Australian students must go more than half-way with overseas students' because of linguistic and cultural difficulties, or that there was 'too great a tendency for similar nationalities to stick together. More social activities [should be] planned by both Australians and overseas students'.

Australians tended to assume that 'to know us is to love us', but there were aspects of Australian life that jarred on overseas students and especially those from Asia. Australian informality could look like lack of respect, especially for older students; the free and easy relations between the sexes shocked some and Australia's traditional lack of reverence for authority puzzled others. Cross-cultural understanding was complicated by the fact that the overseas students tended to be postgraduates and the Australians undergraduates often in their junior years. Mrs McCutcheon, who could combine gentility with plain speaking, remarked that some of the students from Hong Kong thought that Australians talked too much. She also reported the observation of a female Japanese resident, who remarked: 'Ours is maybe a less developed country but maybe we are more developed in human relationships. In childhood we are taught courtesy and pleasantness; in your shops so few smile or are polite. I think they deprive themselves of pleasure in their daily work.'

In her report based on two months' residence in the House in early 1972, Irene Prescott of the Berkeley IH, candid in reporting the good and the bad news, remarked that some overseas students found 'Australian students have little interest in them, and that the Aussies are self-centred'. To counter this, she recommended that there be a more critical selection of Australian residents and that those with an interest in Asia or Africa be given preference; also that some of the IH staff should also come from those regions. One recommendation speaks volumes about the cultural divide: that there should be 'less emphasis on alcoholic beverages, especially at parties'. As always, bringing cultures together made people as aware of differences as of similarities — which, after all, was one of the purposes of IH.

Indeed, Rosalie McCutcheon, who spoke with authority on such matters, thought that, if anything, there was sometimes a tendency to be too bland, to gloss over the differences between cultures. 'If there has been a particular weakness in relationships and interaction in the House', she remarked at the tenth anniversary dinner, 'I wonder if it had been the tendency to be too nice to each other, to avoid giving offence ... Some members of the House have doubtless left it almost unscathed by any real, clashing interaction with other minds or any effort to understand.'

There were, all the same, many good news stories that showed that the IH formula could work. The Alumni Newsletter for December 1973, for example, includes a brief letter from a Korean former resident, Suk-chong Cho: 'I never receive the SUIHAA Newsletter without being reminded of my happy days in Australia.' He was my room mate in 1972 (and we continued to exchange Christmas cards for many years afterwards), so I had some sense of the difficulties as well as the opportunities he faced in coming to terms with Australia. Above all, there was the problem of language, even though he was an English teacher who had come to the University of Sydney and the House to complete a diploma in teaching English as a second language along with a number of other compatriots. The temptation for this little band of mature-age, married Korean teachers (who had had to leave behind their families) to form a little ghetto must have been strong. As a teacher in the Confucian tradition he was quite shocked at what he saw in Australian schools and the lack of respect that teachers received. The Australian informality with first names also jarred and he gently put me right on what name I should use; only his wife would use the equivalent of his first name. Hence if someone left a message he would faithfully pass it on with a note saying that 'Mr or Miss So-and-So' had called by. But he overcame the linguistic and cultural divides to complete his qualification (which later opened up a post in a tertiary institution) and remained in touch with the IH alumni.

The White Australia policy might have been in its death throes in the early seventies, but attitudes in the broader Australian community did not change overnight. In contrast to today, when internationalisation is so much a part of Australian university life (and finances), overseas students tended to stand out and to be subject to attention whether for good or ill. There had been a strong sense for some time that it was important for Australia's future in the region that overseas students, from South-east Asia particularly, should return home with, as the *Murray Report* put it in 1957, 'an intimate knowledge of Australians, of Australian thought and of Australian ideals'. Convincing some Australians of this took some doing and the internationally-minded members of Rotary — a body that specifies as one of its avenues of service 'the development of international understanding and goodwill between people of different nations' — reported that some of their fellow countrymen were less than enthusiastic about parting with their cash to help overseas students by building IH.

In the view of one Japanese student, Tatsuo Aoyama, who recorded his impressions in the IHMA magazine for 1978, Australia still seemed closely tied to the remnants of empire, since 'The majority of white Australians seem to be nostalgic towards Britain as "God Save the Queen" shows'. Australia's economy also seemed rather backward-looking since reliance on the exporting of raw materials 'does not indicate an industrialised country'. Good-humouredly he concluded, however, 'Australia gives me a bit of a hard time in some ways, but I love this country and have learnt much'.

In 1969 there were about 700 overseas students at the University of Sydney and throughout the 1970s the number remained at about that level. Usually during that decade the University of Sydney accepted something like 300 a year, but the number could fluctuate. In 1976 it fell to 70, with the result that IH had to change its admission policy and, for the first time, allow in first-year Australian students. In addition, to boost numbers, one floor was also remodelled to allow for self-catering residents. Despite this brief dip the need for residential places for overseas students remained strong and provided the rationale for the steady expansion of the House over the course of the seventies.

The East Wing, from Maze Crescent, 1971

The opening of the East Wing in 1972 created an additional 22 rooms (eight of them twin), thus expanding the existing student population of 120 by a further 30. It also included two common rooms and a staff flat. East Wing rooms were regarded as particularly desirable and were much sought after: among their other attractions was the fact that there was a bathroom for each pair of rooms, instead of the more communal bathrooms in the multi-storied residence. They were built that way partly with a view to turning them into married accommodation if necessary. The *University News* of 29 March 1972 reported that it was built so as not to 'inhibit the siting of the second multi-storey residential wing, for which funds are again being sought' — but IH lost much of this possible site to such near neighbours as the Seymour Centre and the Architecture Faculty, so the second high-rise building never eventuated (which perhaps helped keep IH's numbers at a more manageable level).

The East Wing was, however, followed in 1979 by the Elkin Wing which accommodated another 30 students in fourteen single study bedrooms and four suites. It was built over two levels, each of which had a kitchenette and sitting rooms. Like the East Wing, it deliberately included double rooms since, to the surprise of the Director, quite a few students actually preferred a shared room (common practice in the USA, for example). By contrast, there were only a few twin rooms in the main residential block. Both the East and Elkin wings widened the House's style of accommodation to include some married students (including their children), which added to the character of IH (and further differentiated it from other student residences on campus). Overall if there was underlying design to the expansion of IH it was to provide students with a variety of types of accommodation and this was later to be taken further with the units in the Maze Building.

A very different sort of building was the log cabin, erected in the Belanglo State Forest, south of the picturesque old coaching town of Berrima, about 200 kilometres from Sydney. It was inspired by a visit in 1977 by the then Assistant Director, Mollie Burns, to IH Berkeley, during which she spent some time at its Lodestar International Centre in the Sierra Mountains. She prompted the Director and the Council to get behind a scheme to erect something comparable and the Forestry Commission was persuaded to provide a site at a peppercorn rent. Those two great supporters of IH over the years, Ian Hudson and Brian Farmer, did much to further the venture — the former by arranging for the import of the prefabricated log kit from Tasmania and the latter (an engineer) by providing much of the design and hands-on plumbing and electrical work. Much of the manual labour was provided by the

A weekend work party, Belanglo Log Cabin, 1979
(Brian Farmer, back row, far left; Graeme de Graaff, front row, far left)

students themselves, who were often transported in the House van. When the place opened in 1979, it provided accommodation for twelve people who, in winter, could snuggle around a pot-bellied stove. Other visitors included the kangaroos, rabbits and native birds that came out in the evening.

The Belanglo Log Cabin served, and has continued to serve, as a base for visiting many of the local scenic attractions, among them the Wombeyan Caves. As time went on, its facilities became less basic. The pit-toilet — fondly known as 'Wescombe Manor', in tribute to the work contributed to its construction by Roger Wescombe — was upgraded to a flush model with septic tank, a move hastened by Forestry Commission concerns about possible pollution. Mollie Burns later donated funds for a solar hot water system, thus rendering obsolete the previous cold-water 'bush shower'.

The Log Cabin came cheap, but generally buildings cost lots of money. Nonetheless, as we have seen, this decade saw the first two of the three extensions to the House, with the East Wing opening in 1972 and the Elkin Wing in 1979. (The Maze Building would 'complete' the project in 1985.) That new buildings came in such rapid succession was a surprise to many, including those members of the Council who had had to work so long and hard to raise the funds for the first stage.

When the Director first raised the idea of an East Wing with the Council, his proposal was met with a mixture of disbelief and even the trace of a weary groan. It was firmly agreed that there was no chance of a new Rotary fund-raising appeal. From the University, Harold Maze looked surprised but could not hide the gleam in his eye. A. P. Elkin, backed his Senate ally (Maze) and a Director with whom he was coming to form a similar relationship.

Doreen Langley had no hesitation in encouraging the Council to let the Director have his head. She knew that he was endeavouring to put into practice the doctrine of Davis McCaughey, the much-respected head of Ormond College, Melbourne (and, later, Governor of Victoria). The accepted wisdom was that the optimum number for a University hall of residence was 240! That meant that the number at International House could be doubled, while many of the overhead operating costs would not increase at all. (Pass the 240-resident mark and, it was maintained, serious and expensive additions would be needed in the administrative structure.)

The Director had calculations on the back of an envelope which showed that, with no increase in residents' fees, the full cost of an east wing could be borrowed and the loan repaid in twelve years from the operating economies of scale. He also argued that a new type of adaptable accommodation was needed — for senior academics, possibly married students and the resident Assistant Director.

An approach for assistance was, of course, made to the Universities Commission, which controlled the federal funds, but after the original grants for the Rotunda and residence, International House never received government help for building. (An officer once remarked: 'You seem to be able to manage without our money.') The wing was built. Because of the serious inflation at that time, the fixed interest loan was paid off in six years, half the allocated time; hence the claim that the East Wing was 'the wing that inflation built'.

That had been so easy that the Council was happy to do it all again for a south wing. This time some Councillors thought that there was space for a public appeal. Others were opposed to bringing in professional fund-raisers and this was not done. Inflation was kind again and the debt was soon paid off.

Financially, then, IH was increasingly thrown back on its own resources. Government was less and less involved and, after contributing so much to the establishment of IH with a long and rather bruising campaign, Rotary by then also had other priorities — though individual Rotarians continued to be very generous. Thus fund-raising during these years could be very hard work. One scheme, introduced in the late seventies to raise money for what became the Elkin Wing, was to allow people who donated five thousand dollars and over to name a room. Lesser donations of five hundred dollars brought with them the privilege of donors becoming Affiliated Members of International House who would receive invitations to House functions and copies of the annual report.

One person who took the lead in fund-raising for the expansion of the House was the Rotarian, Ian Hudson, one of IH's longest-serving and generous Council members and Chairs. During the 1970s and thereafter, he pushed for the expansion of the House. As he put it, he felt it was important to 'use up the very valuable property which was given to us by the University'. No doubt it was in his mind that what the University could give it could also take away. In his view, 'the function of the Council of our International House is one of continuous fund-raising because apart from this the Council have very little to do'.

Not all Council members might have agreed completely with this and no doubt the volume of business for Council waxed and waned, but it was a sign that IH was travelling well that not too much was being asked of its Council. It was an indication, too, that the University was content to let the House and its Director get on with things without much interference. The University was, of course, represented on Council since IH was a hall of residence of the University (as one was reminded by the fact that the House then used University stationery). Indeed, the 22 or so members of Council included, *ex officio*, the Chancellor and the Vice-Chancellor, though they usually nominated representatives.

There were also generally at least three representatives of Rotary, an ongoing indication of their importance not only in the founding of the House, but their continuing interest in its welfare. Rotarians (and especially those connected with the Newtown branch) provided overseas students with hospitality and gave personal donations to assist with House causes, such as the improvement of the library.

The IH Council also included three student representatives, though in the politically-charged aftermath of the 1975 dismissal of the Whitlam government some students were inclined to satirise its proceedings. One such student wrote in the IHMA magazine for 1978 that at IH 'We have our own GG [Governor-General/Graeme de Graaff]' and his 'upper house Council are closely allied with the ruling aristocracy of the academic world'; the lower house (the IHMA committee and the like), by contrast, he saw as holding little power.

Along with the Rotarians, another group of people who were a part of IH from its foundation, and continued as an active force in the 1970s, were the members of the Women's Committee. At its peak it had about 60 members and its goals were not only to raise money for the House but also to provide the residents with contact with Australian families (including morning teas for newcomers). One of the ways that funds were raised was by establishing the House shop. By 1970 it was decided that the running of the shop in the evenings could be handed over to IHMA, but the women volunteers kept it open during lunch hours, providing not only a community service but also a friendly ear for residents, especially those from abroad. Their fund-raising ventures also often added to the cultural ambience of IH with concerts, including many at which the distinguished opera singer Lauris Elms (aka Mrs de Graaff) performed.

In 1977, some eight women of the first committee convened in 1966 by Kathleen O'Neil were still active and they could look back on a diverse range of activities, including dinners with Margaret Whitlam and the Duchess of Bedford, together with a number of Four Seasons Fairs at which exotic objects were sold and international food provided. These produced the wherewithal for a number of improvements around the House including curtains for the Wool Room, coffee room and television room. The Wool Room also benefited from the purchase of a piano, a PA system and double glazing and residents who wished to use the roof garden now had garden furniture at their disposal. Later committees provided curtains for the Log Cabin and the Elkin Wing. Overall, their aim, as Kathleen O'Neil said, was 'to help provide the House with things it needed which could not be provided through the ordinary financial arrangements of the House itself'.

As time went by there emerged another natural grouping that was not resident but yet had a strong interest in IH: the alumni — but incorporating them in the life of the House took some time. Those from the early years of the House had strong ties and naturally wanted to maintain their link with an institution that had loomed so large in their formative years. It was, however, in the nature of things that a young institution, preoccupied with consolidation and growth, had not thought too deeply about those that had left. Some of the early alumni felt rather under-appreciated. Its 1972 Newsletter included some strong words from the President of SUIHAA: 'The place of the Alumni Association and its relevance to International House is often questioned, both privately and publicly.' Such thoughts were prompted in part by the lack of mention of the alumni in the second report of Council — something, continued the President Frank Schaer, that 'raises the question of our part, in the concept and ideal of the House'.

Another problem was to be an ongoing one for the alumni association: that of generational change. As the early, fairly tightly-knit graduates became more and more preoccupied with careers and family responsibilities there was something of a hiatus in others coming forward to take the place of the first alumni as office-bearers in SUIHAA. The 1975 Newsletter expressed the committee's concern 'at the lack of activity and interest on the local scene, as evidenced by the poor attendance at AGMs'. Among Mrs McCutcheon's many other contributions to the life of the House was her help in maintaining the morale of the alumni, in part by offering practical suggestions. One such was to integrate them more into the activities of the House by asking distinguished alumni back to give informal talks.

Thanks to the dedicated efforts of a number of alumni, the association was kept afloat during these years and by 1980 had achieved a major breakthrough with more formal recognition by Council. It not only acknowledged the importance of SUIHAA, as detailed in the next chapter, but also decided to provide the association with tangible support.

Within the House, then, the seventies was a time of consolidation and growth. It was also a time for establishing which of the ideals that had inspired its foundation could be practically realised. Some, such as the outreach beyond the hall of residence to the University and the larger population of overseas students in the state, had to be downgraded, if not abandoned altogether. But as a place where Australians and overseas students could live and study together it was very much a going concern — even if the hope 'that brotherhood may prevail' had to be qualified by the realisation that brotherhood did not mean sameness.

Outside the House in the larger world of the University and Australian society more generally, the decade was one of considerable change. In many ways it carried on the 'cultural revolution' of the sixties, a feature of the Western world generally which came late to Australia. The traditional mortar of society in the form of the values instilled by church, family and respect for hierarchy was very much under question — in part because there were simply a lot more young people about because of the post-war baby boom. Traditional gender roles were also called into question by the women's liberation movement and by the increasing numbers of women going on to higher education — by the end of the seventies, the University of Sydney was enrolling as many women as men and, in keeping with the changing mores, classes were less didactic and more given over to discussion.

More broadly, Australia's sense of national identity was also changing fast as the ties of empire were weakened by Britain's entry into the European Community in 1975; and the election of the Whitlam Labor government in 1972 challenged many of the assumptions that had accompanied the long rule of conservative governments. Of particular relevance to International House were Australia's changing relations with Asia: the Vietnam War and its aftermath, the killing fields of Cambodia, and the recognition of what was known as the mainland Chinese government — which followed within a few days of the election of the Labor government on 2 December 1972. (A small ripple from this tidal change in Australia's foreign relations was the arrival in the House in 1975 of a few students from the People's Republic of China for a brief visit and later, in 1979, for a more extended stay by nine such students.)

Such seismic changes rolled over IH, causing remarkably little upheaval. Perhaps there was less to rebel against there: it lacked the weight of tradition found in the colleges, with their church affiliations and symbolic recognition of hierarchy with high tables and the like. One of the functions of colleges had been to control the relations between the sexes with gate passes and curfews, but these had never existed at IH. From the start, IH had recognised the importance of having residents of both genders and including both women and men in senior roles in the administration, as instanced by Rosalie McCutcheon's importance in the shaping of the House. It is easy to forget in the light of today's attitudes how momentous a step it was for IH to offer mixed accommodation from the outset, being the first to decide to be co-residential. One of the key members of the planning committee that established the House, as already noted, was Doreen Langley, who, as the Principal of Women's College, naturally had gender issues very much on her mind. One of the reasons that Graeme de Graaff was chosen over another candidate for the post of Director was that he, unlike his competitor, had not ignored her at the interview. He also had the advantage of bringing with him his wife, Lauris Elms, who, it was rightly predicted, would play a valuable part in the life of the House.

In IH's early years women and men were to some extent separated since they occupied different floors, with the women on the seventh and the eighth. But around the middle of the decade this separation was eroded. By 1974 the fourth floor was mixed, the seventh floor followed suit the next year and the East and Elkin wings were mixed from the time of their opening. By around 1976 there were only two segregated floors, level 6 (for men) and 8 (for women), and eventually women and men came to share the same living spaces throughout IH. One of the

61

difficulties was to attract overseas women to a co-ed institution and this was one of the reasons why, from its foundation and throughout the 1970s, the population of the House changed little from being one-third women within the basic half-Australian and half-overseas resident mix. The women that were attracted were, however, often some of the more adventurous spirits, willing to try out a new institution, including what was then this novel experiment of having men and women in one residence.

Such co-existence helped women and men to meet regularly in a more companionable, even a domestic, kind of setting than generally prevailed at the time. Predictably the result was quite a few marriages: by 1976 the count had reached something like 45. Mrs McCutcheon attributed this (and the generally higher success rate of these marriages) to the 'freedom of relationships. They saw each other at breakfast, dinner and tea and hammered out ideas'.

Such ideas might well include the changing role of women, an issue on which residents were invited to reflect, for example, at a talk in the mid-seventies by the distinguished anthropologist Margaret Jolly, who spoke in the House on the issue of matriarchy and whether societies were always dominated by men, or could they have been previously dominated by women? As always, a new movement provoked something of a backlash: the IHMA magazine for 1978 included an article acknowledging that 'The female liberation movement has brought many benefits to males', but thought that 'zeal frequently outruns discretion' and suggested that as well as the term 'male chauvinist' there should also be 'female chauvinettes'.

Along with women's liberation, the other movement that most galvanised youth of university age in the early seventies was the war in Vietnam. I remember visiting an IH friend who was on a draft charge in Long Bay Gaol in 1972, when conscription was still very real. It was abolished with the advent of the Whitlam government at the end of that year. A number of residents had been national servicemen in Vietnam and this could provoke heated discussion in the House. Reportedly, one such was asked by a resident if he had shot anyone in Vietnam and when he replied 'Yes', the response was 'Murderer'. Attendance or absence from the moratorium marches could also lead to lively exchanges. Even Mrs McCutcheon was told in no uncertain terms by a member of the office staff that it had been most unbecoming of her to take part in one of these marches.

The presence of US residents added to the temperature of debate. I remember one of them getting very angry at an anti-American discussion over a meal (though when I caught up with him again a few years later at his home in Oklahoma, he was the soul of hospitality). A talk at the House in 1971 by the US Consul prompted a letter of thanks from the then Acting Director, Belinda Dawson, expressing her gratitude for his willingness 'to be the brunt of the attack that seems an inevitable part of US foreign policy'.

In the early seventies there were also still some students who were sponsored by the anti-communist government of South Vietnam who were more loath to enter into debate, but could let one know privately that they felt passionately about the need to protect their country. Some were later to suffer greatly: in 1980 the Director received a letter from a Thai refugee camp from a former resident from Vietnam. She and her son had fled, since 'I could not live in Vietnam freely and happily'. En route she had 'met so many pirates on the ocean, and we have lost all money and things'. Naturally, her hopes were centred on a return to Australia. There were also some students from Cambodia who, as educated people, would in many cases have later perished in the killing fields. One of my memories is of these gentle people holding ballroom dancing classes (then considered a bit old-fashioned or quaint) in the Wool Room — which makes even more poignant the brutal fate that many of them would have later endured.

The 1970s, then, was a heady time and the fact that the House weathered it without too much apparent discord was an indication that its foundations had been laid securely. It is hard now in this global age when equality between men and women is taken for granted to recapture the sense of excitement prompted by the experiment of having overseas and Australian students and men and women living together. Needless to say, sometimes the experiment went flat or even exploded or, more commonly, the ingredients simply did not react as Australians and overseas students sometimes co-existed rather than interacted. Overall, however, there was enough energy and idealism generated by bringing together the different elements to make all the work that had gone into the foundation of International House seem time well spent.

Sources

Once again, I am grateful for the comments of Graeme de Graaff, as also for those of Michael Bennett, Roger Wescombe and my brother, Robert Gascoigne (an IH resident, 1973–74).

IH Archives:

As with the previous chapter, much of this is based on the scrapbooks compiled by Rosemary Berrick. Those relevant to this chapter are Files 1.1, 1.2 and 1.3. Another major source was the Campbell oral history series, transcribed interviews (1.6), in particular, (in order of filing) those with Kathleen O'Neil, Sir Harold Wyndham, Rosalie McCutcheon, W. H. Maze, Pauline Kennedy, Sleath Lowrey, Doreen Langley, Ian Hudson, Geoffrey Howe, Graeme de Graaff and Sir Bernard Freeman.

The material regarding the International Student Centre is catalogued as Files 1.1–10. The 1972 report, 'Review of the Past 5 Years', is located in Box 5.1.20 and the 'Report of the 1980s Committee' is in 8.6 'Alumni Affairs', together with 1980 letters from the Vietnamese alumni.

Alumni Newsletters are kept in the Alumni Room (off the Wool Room).

Publications:

There is surprisingly little published on the history of the University of Sydney during this period, but worth consulting is K. Cable, C. Turney and U. Bygott, *Australia's First. A Pictorial History of the University of Sydney 1850–1990* (Sydney, 1990).

Some useful background was also provided by Lauris Elms's autobiography, *The Singing Elms* (Sydney, 2001).

Chapter Four

The 1980s

Roger Wescombe

In the English-speaking world, the 1980s was a notable decade for the political right. Ronald Reagan was President of the USA from 1980 to 1988, and was succeeded by the first George Bush. Margaret Thatcher was Prime Minister of the United Kingdom for the whole decade. In both those countries neo-classical economic theory dominated policy-making and, at least until share markets plummeted in October 1987, it was fashionable to preach that 'greed is good'. The US led a widespread boycott of the 1980 Moscow Olympics in reprisal, of all things, for the USSR invasion of Afghanistan. In the first half of the decade, especially, there was a strong awareness of the dangers of nuclear war between the then superpowers, heightened by the shooting down of Korean Airlines flight KAL007 by a Soviet military plane in 1983. The status of the USSR as a technological leader was diminished when Chernobyl blew up in 1986 and by the time the Berlin Wall fell in 1989 it was clear that the USA was the sole superpower. In 1989, the People's Republic of China attracted international condemnation for the incident which became widely known as the Tiananmen Square Massacre. In the world of science, the AIDS virus was discovered in 1984, the Human Genome Project commenced in 1988 and cold fusion was discovered and then undiscovered in 1989.

In our own part of the world, a Labor Australian government, itself heavily influenced by neo-classical economic theory, was elected in 1983; the Greenpeace ship 'Rainbow Warrior' was sunk by French secret service operatives in New Zealand in 1985; Corazon Aquino came to power in a peaceful 'people's revolution' in the Philippines in 1986; and non-indigenous Australians celebrated the 200th anniversary of their settlement of Australia in 1988. Australian government commitment to multiculturalism as the basis for relationships between its ethnic groupings, which had commenced in the 1970s, grew to the point that in 1988 there was formal government support for the maintenance of people's individual cultural heritage, including their language and religion, and for the removal of barriers of race, ethnicity, culture, religion, language, gender and place of birth. Support for multiculturalism in the 1980s appeared to come from all political parties represented in the national parliament.

The federal Labor government made major changes to policy on tertiary education. By the end of the decade many tertiary institutions had merged and universities and Colleges of Advanced Education had been combined into a 'unified national system', based on claims that this would provide more efficient use of public resources. In 1987 Australian students were required to meet part of the cost of their education by paying a Higher Education Administrative Charge which was to be gradually increased and later re-named the Higher Education Contribution Scheme.

The change in policy relating to overseas students was equally dramatic. At the beginning of the eighties, overseas students were seen largely as an aid issue, involving help to developing countries and the expansion of Australian influence in neighbouring countries and South-east Asia. This type of assistance continued throughout the decade for students specifically nominated by their governments for aid. After 1979, however, private overseas students were required to pay an Overseas Student Charge and this gradually increased until, by 1988, it was 55 per cent of the average full cost of a university place.

In 1984 two major official reports on overseas students were released: the *Goldring Report* and the *Jackson Report*. The former argued for a continuation of Overseas Student Charge arrangements as a commitment to education in the region, while the latter focussed on the potential of Australian tertiary education as an export industry competing with its equivalents in the USA, UK and Canada. The *Jackson Report,* with its neo-classical economic preoccupations, was the more influential, with the result that in 1985 the Australian government, apparently seeing the economic value of education as an export industry, decided to introduce a new category of overseas students: those who would pay the full cost of their education. By 1988, almost all universities were recruiting or planning to recruit full-fee-paying students from abroad. Thus 'user pays' and 'market rules' principles were almost as thoroughly adopted in Australian tertiary education as they were in Thatcher's Britain or Reagan's USA.

These events in the wider world echoed through the daily thoughts of IH residents and administrators. Sometimes the influence was consciously managed in the House program. Concern in the 1980s with the conflict between the USA and the Soviet Union, for example, is discernible in the printed record. IHMA Sports Committee Chairman, Stephen White, in 1980 ironically linked the House Games he was organising to the boycott of the Moscow Olympic Games, describing the House Games as 'the IHMA's small but vital contribution to the Olympic boycott'. The Director's comment in the 1980 annual magazine had the sombre conclusion: 'In International House we live in the future, or there will be none.' The Alumni Association's Foundation Day Address in 1983 was on the subject 'World War III', given by Dr Keith Suter. And after the Korean airliner was shot down that year, with the possibility of escalating hostilities from such an event, the House program included a model United Nations Security Council meeting, dealing with the hypothetical, accidental deployment of a US guided missile and the ensuing international panic. The meeting was preceded by Wool Room discussions of nuclear strategy and visits to embassies in Canberra by some fifteen residents.

The eighties also saw the development of academic interest in 'peace studies'. Students of Sydney University's Department of Social Work set up a Staff–Student Committee for the Introduction of Peace Studies, with the cheerful acronym 'SSCIPS'. Comprising the Social Work students, Social Work lecturer Ms Mary Lane, Government lecturer Dr Peter King and, from International House, myself, the committee reached the stage where it was ready to launch a formal entity. At a public symposium on peace studies in the Wool Room in 1986, sponsored by International House, the University's Professor of Social Work, Stuart Rees, moved that a centre be set up to promote formal peace and conflict studies in the University. In due course the Centre for Peace and Conflict Studies was created. It went on to develop postgraduate degree programs and to spawn the prestigious Sydney Peace Prize, awarded in subsequent years to such internationally recognised figures as Muhammad Yunnus, Archbishop Desmond Tutu, Mary Robinson and Hanan Ashrawi.

By the 1980s, an era of exceptional scientific advancement had enabled many to enjoy, and take for granted, the fruits of science and technology. Rather than rejoicing in these advances and seeking to further promote the science that had enriched them, many became impatient with science and sought a short cut to scientific discovery by means of 'new age' remedies that were 'holistic', 'organic' or 'natural'. More seriously, but arguably in the same direction, was the interest from a variety of serious scientists in the possibility of a 'new scientific paradigm' that would view the world in other than mechanistic terms. In the late eighties, the University of Sydney's Centre for the Human Aspects of Science and Technology focussed on the work of Ilya Prigogine, Isabelle Stengers and Fritjof Capra in this connection and sponsored a major 1990 public lecture by the English biologist, Rupert Sheldrake, whose research was extensively into the paranormal. International House became involved in such matters in 1986 when Dr Bevan Reid, in the University's Queen Elizabeth II Research Institute, decided to promote creativity in the Institute's medical research by having a highly regarded Australian artist, Robert Pope, paint canvasses in the laboratory where the research was proceeding. Accommodation was booked for Robert Pope in IH. Bevan Reid described the research in which he was involved as 'creative physics' and he gave a talk in International House and challenged a number of the House's science graduates to consider his research. During the evening Reid met a number of residents' arguments with Hamlet's dictum: 'There are more things in heaven and earth, than are dreamt of in your philosophy.' After that, and a few visits to his laboratory, the residents remained unconvinced and joined other members of the University's scientific community who denounced Reid's research. One IH resident, George Roumeliotis, expressed his scepticism about the research in an item for the House magazine on 'phunny physics'.

The idea of anti-discrimination legislation as a means of regulating behaviour towards stigmatised or disadvantaged minority groups grew internationally in the 1970s and 1980s. The first New South Wales anti-discrimination legislation came into force in 1977 and was extensively enlarged in the early eighties. It forbade discrimination on the basis of race, sex, marital status, physical impairment, intellectual impairment and homosexuality in a variety of specified contexts. Since the sincerely held ideals of International House had as their central tenet the idea that people of different races and cultures should be able to co-exist peacefully, productively and in many senses equally, it seemed unlikely that International House would face a problem; and yet it did. Indeed International House found itself one of the first institutions affected when a resident accused the House of discriminating against him as a disabled person by refusing to allow him to mask the corridor lights outside his study-bedroom and to have a range of other special provisions, including special catering. The House was an economical and social success partly because of the control the Director exercised over the physical maintenance of the building and which the Council, including IHMA members, expected him to exercise over such matters as catering. Here was a challenge to the Director's right to manage the House in accordance with the arrangements set by the Council. The law had moved ahead of International House, allocating rights which this most humanitarian of institutions was reluctant to recognise. In the event, the matter was settled by negotiation, without a court or tribunal ruling, and the resident left the House.

As well as being the era for the resurgence of neo-classical economic theory, the eighties was also a decade of managerialism, the application of that neo-classical theory, in a formal way, to the management of both private sector and public sector organisations. The application of neo-classical economic theory to institutions such as universities was well under way in the 1980s. Graeme de Graaff wrote in favour of what later became known as the 'commodification of education' in the 1983 House magazine:

> There is a big market in Asia for education. It should be developed. Thousands of people from foreign countries want to buy the education which Australian Universities and Colleges of Advanced Education sell. All of them can afford it... . We have a good product. It is wanted. Let us sell it. Let us develop the market. At present we allow ourselves to think of overseas student education as though it were part of some charity for the needy. If we get clear that it is not, we will help ourselves. We may even go on to help others.

The residents of International House were accustomed, through their IHMA representatives, to thinking about cost/benefit analyses of House facilities, so there was nothing alien about those elements of neo-classical theory. Managerialist concerns may be discernible, however, in a frequent concern in IHMA committees in the 1980s with constitutional reform and a confidence that this would lead to efficiencies. In 1983 IHMA produced an Annual Report eleven pages (not including financial accounts) long. In his introduction, the President, Charles Latimer, noted with evident satisfaction: '1983 primarily was notable for the "good management" and balanced financial aspects. The portfolio system introduced in 1980 worked, not brilliantly, but satisfactorily and the Central Co-ordinators Committee enjoyed a harmonious working relationship at almost all times.'

With a thoroughness not approached in other IHMA reports, this one went on to catalogue: the allocation of over 100 committee and group positions to various residents; the attendance of committee members at IHMA committee meetings; the findings of two Review Committees; reorganisation of records and archives; University recognition (of the IHMA); college liaison; surveys on catering and program respectively; liaison with the Alumni Association; contact with other Australian International Houses; an extensive finance and services report; and reports on entertainment, publications, sports, shop, facilities, food liaison, telephone roster, floor representatives and liaison and representation.

There were other instances of international issues being picked up in House activities: in 1984, Professors Jack Goldring, Derek Tribe and Helen Hughes gave a three-part Foundation Day Address on the developments in Australian overseas student policy referred to above; in 1985 there was a guest speaker on South Africa's Apartheid as that policy reached its final few years of life; the 1986 International Year of Peace was celebrated in a series of lunchtime Wool Room talks on peace and justice issues; the trial of the drug couriers Barlow and Chambers in Malaysia led to guest speakers on crime and punishment issues and excursions to the Supreme Court and the Emu Plains prison; and an alumnus, Nick Stuart, visited the House in 1989 as a guest speaker about his experiences in China during the student revolts.

Thus was a range of international influences reflected in the program. In the meantime the full range of IH roles was being played out at 96 City Road; at any given time International House was playing the following roles:

1. provider of bed and/or board and study facilities to a number of students and others;
2. creator of the environment in which a number of overseas and Australian students mature socially;
3. provider of social support to members of its community;
4. source of an exercise in multicultural living;
5. educator of its members about international affairs; and
6. source of some beneficial influence on the wider world … spreading the light.

The Director, of course, oversaw all the above areas as well as managing the House's relationship with the University. The resident Assistant Director had particular responsibilities in relation to 1, 2, 3 and 4. The IHMA had particular responsibilities in relation to 2, 3, 4 and 5. And the Director of the program, when there was one, had particular responsibilities in relation to 2, 4, 5 and 6. Those in the position of Senior Resident likewise had responsibilities spread across a wide range of these roles. In such a structure, each person or body faces pressure from their respective constituency to show they are achieving; each is dependent on the same complex entity, the spirit of the community, for their success; each can have a different sense of what that spirit is and what it needs to be for their initiatives to thrive; and each can have a different sense of how they can best generate the spirit they seek.

The need for co-operation between parties with such overlapping boundaries of responsibility and the potential for at least mild friction in such a subtle business is obvious. The nature and quality of this co-operation varied over the decade, reflecting the different personalities of the protagonists. Soon after assuming responsibility for the program in 1982, I underestimated the pressure IHMA felt to achieve and to demonstrate achievement. The resulting dissonance hung around interminably and was behind much of the 1983 friction between the IHMA and 'the administration' referred to later in this chapter. On the other hand, the Assistant Directors, Pauline Kennedy (Program) and Rosemary Fisher (Residence), reported an exceptionally comfortable and exuberant relationship with the IHMA and its Chairperson, Geoff Heenan, in 1989 and participation in the program by the Bursar Elizabeth Morris and receptionist Shama Abraham as well! Throughout the 1980s, under both Graeme de Graaff and Geoffrey Andrews, co-operation between staff members, at least, was built by means of a weekly staff dinner in the Director's dining room. It is certainly most comfortable for everyone when the engines of House life are in tune with one another, though it is difficult to know whether dissonance or consonance of this type is more productive of quality education.

During the 1980s, and throughout the House's whole history, the resident Assistant Director position remained one of the constants of the International House organisation. The position was called 'Assistant to the Director' in 1987 and 1988 but that appears to have made little difference to its nature. The Assistant Directors throughout the decade were: Joan Rowlands (1979–1980), Toshiko Mori and Youngsok Song (1981–1983), Julia Arnold (1983–1986), Carol Carney (1987–1988) and Rosemary Fisher (1989–1991). Rosemary Fisher provided a simple summary of the resident Assistant Director's responsibilities and dilemmas in her contribution to the Director's Annual Report to Council of October 1989:

> An Assistant Director (Resident) whose role (as I see and perform it) is largely one of liaison; attempting to bring and hold together the House community; to act as agent/medium and to keep channels of communication and action open. Adults cannot be dragooned into having 'House spirit'. Such feelings arise from fellowship and friendship... The facilitating of resident interaction occurs also on a more informal basis — in a series of floor parties held in the Assistant Director's flat, in the Women's Committee Welcome Picnic and in the Faculty Suppers. The Assistant Director acts as a first — and sometimes only — House contact with transients and works with the conferences. The position involves the simple mechanics of housekeeping, the organising of the annual House photograph and conducting fire drills until the residents get

the evacuation procedures right! There are places for the Assistant Director on the House and Finance Committee, as a visitor on Council, on the Food, Alumni and Bursary committees. It all adds up to a matter of performance and accessibility. There is always a shifting tightrope to walk between firmness and friendliness, one's initiative and one's imposition, one's person and persona.

When Toshiko Mori and Youngsok Song left after two-and-a-half years, the Director reported to Council:

The longer an Assistant Director stays in the job and the better she is at it, the more that is asked of her and the more difficult it becomes! Young Sok and Toshiko did much for the residents in their time here. Many people were very sad to see them go. I am deeply grateful to them for the support they gave to the House and to me.

Similarly, towards the end of Julia Arnold's two-and-a-half years as Assistant Director, the Director again paid tribute to the multi-faceted and vital nature of this role:

The Assistant Director continued to ensure that the House was a people-oriented place, and not one of the aforementioned transients missed her welcoming reception. Many went out of their way to comment on how uniquely friendly they found the House. The Assistant Director's support for residents is unobtrusive, vital and expressed in a wide variety of ways from handling breakdowns to helping a departing resident to establish a flat for his arriving family.

It is not surprising that there should have been such a turnover in resident Assistant Directors. The position is so engrossing, so compelling and ultimately so gruelling that, despite the considerable psychic rewards, it is difficult to sustain for more than two years. Having an outside job, as the above-named Assistant Directors did, limits the intensity of the experience, but involves an unsustainable workload. Essential to the effective management of the House and the sanity of the resident Assistant Director, once the House extended beyond the North (original) wing and the East Wing, was the position of Senior Resident. Each year one or more residents in this position enjoyed the benefit of reduced fees and, in return, performed both routine and community-building tasks for which the resident Assistant Director had insufficient time. Senior Residents in the 1980s included Greg Bird, Murray Baker, Donna Priol, 'PH' Phongsavan, Toru Aoyama and Iqbal Qureshi.

The IHMA was often an outstanding institution in the 1980s. Sometimes it had a 'Chairman' (irrespective of the gender of the incumbent), sometimes it had a 'Chairperson', and in 1983 it had a 'President'. The Chairperson (by which term all three are denoted), as in earlier years, would meet with the Director frequently, usually weekly. This in itself was a significant educational opportunity for the Chairperson who had the benefit of the Director's perception of the House and also of how to be an effective leader of IHMA. The Chairpersons were members of the IH Council and usually reported to each Council meeting and in the House magazine at the end of the year. The Council membership of the Chairperson and up to two IHMA members ensured that the residents, through their representatives, were seriously involved in the major decisions of the eighties, including the design of the Maze Building and the appointment of a new Director. In 1989, consistent with Geoffrey Andrews's view that the House should spread its expertise widely, the IHMA President, Geoff Heenan, and its Secretary, Tanya Golding, attended the student conference running parallel with the Heads of Colleges conference and wrote a paper on the provision Australian colleges made for overseas students.

To judge from the tone of the end-of-year magazines, the IHMA was an enthusiastic contributor to the social life of the House and the achievement of its educational objectives. The Director's 'Word' in the 1980 House magazine refers to his longstanding philosophy of 'freedom with responsibility'. The residents did indeed take on a lot of responsibility, institutionally as well as in everyday communication with fellow residents. Their IHMA representatives were in continuous interaction with their constituency whenever they were in the House; they had the responsibility of meeting as a committee and in sub-committees, meeting weekly with the Director, meeting monthly as members of the House and Finance Committee and meeting four or so times annually as members of the IH Council. As members of activity sub-committees they had the additional tasks of creating a range of House events.

At the end of her stay in 1980, while relieving Joan Rowlands during some holidays, Rosalie McCutcheon wrote positively in the House magazine of the effectiveness of the IHMA and House administration and of the exciting new acquisitions, the furnishings, the House bus and the Belanglo Log Cabin:

I have been quite amazed by the relaxed atmosphere and relative quietness of the House. The dining room, in spite of so many new residents, is so well organised as to be uncrowded, the green of living plants inside the House and out is restful, the whole place looks so cared for. I realise it is 3rd Term when 'everybody works' and, too, that I have not moved around in the House very much. But my impression is that an efficient IHMA Committee as well as a remarkable staff keeps the House running smoothly at all levels and at the same time provides for an exciting and diverse program.

Little did I expect that in 3rd Term I'd share in a Ball, a Musical Variety Evening, a Fellows' Dinner, and an Alumni Dinner, all in the Wool Room, which, by the way, strikes me as being strangely quiet and unused during the day. I was quite enchanted by a visit to Belanglo Log Cabin and hope you all experience it during your time of residence. Travelling in the House Bus that took some of us to the Winifred West Schools in Mittagong and Bowral's tulips was a new experience. What a boon that Bus is!

Her concern, however, was that the House may become too comfortable, too given to the thoughtless enjoyment of these new indulgences:

As I write I call to mind something I once quoted at a House Dinner. I had read, concerning a distinguished man that it was characteristic of him that he always tried to discover antagonisms and to reconcile them... to understand ideas that he'd normally be inclined to reject. Please think about this as it applies to living in IH. If it should lack the hard thinking and disturbing clash of ideas, and the reconciliations for which it provides, IH could become too relaxed and pleasant falling short of its defined and undefined goals.

It is in the nature of disturbing clashes of ideas that they do not appear in the guise one expects. In 1982 and more so in 1983, there was such a clash of ideas about the IHMA and the House administration and governance. The existence of such a clash is not really surprising. In a university hall of residence there is an obvious potential for conflict between residents and management. In such conflict the

Kathleen O'Neil,
retiring as Convenor of the
Women's Committee, 1989

IHMA officers, as the residents' elected leaders, would be the obvious leaders of opposition, if not its instigators. In 1983 the IHMA 'President's Report' in the House magazine for that year enumerates a range of IHMA achievements and proceeds to the following: '1983 was not without its problems — yet again disputes with the Deputy Director arose which was unfortunately unavoidable. The Building Committee changed Stage IV's plans again and again and the Council of International House again showed it knew little about the House itself.' The rancour apparent in this statement had greatly diminished a year later, so that in the magazine of 1984 the Chairman, Virginia Teodosio, wrote with a sense of satisfaction: 'Obviously things must have worked this year as there has been that sense of "belonging" which has made everything to do with the House run smoothly. With the support and inspiration of everyone, the excitement and opportunities available in a place like International House have been realised.'

Such oscillations in atmosphere were summed up when the then Director, Graeme de Graaff, wrote in the 1985 House magazine:

> An atmosphere had developed which was not the happiest or most productive. That was an atmosphere of confrontationalism. A less appropriate model could scarcely be imagined, since the residents, the IHMA the staff, and the Council and its committees all have a common aim, purpose and ideal. There is no doubt that an inappropriate model has gone.

...That the House is now a happier place in which to live, and getting on with its real business, is a reason for real satisfaction. The work of the 1985 Committee under Richard [Andrews]'s chairmanship, building on the groundwork which they inherited from Virginia Teodosio, deserves praise on two levels. It has been an excellent Committee which has given the House a first class year, and it has helped restore mutual respect and confidence.

Two years further on we find the IHMA Chairman, Rico Liu,writing of Graeme de Graaff's newly-appointed successor that: 'As well as the financial support, Mr Andrews's idea of running the House in an informal way with minimal interference, gave us a chance to create an environment which best suits the residents.' It was a sentiment voiced even more forcefully in the last House magazine for the eighties, in which the IHMA Chairperson remarked on the extent to which 'the Director and IHMA had an extremely constructive relationship in 1989, mainly due to Mr Andrews's concern for the welfare of the residents, and his willingness to receive the many (some quite radical) suggestions that were provided'. 'We are fortunate', he wrote, 'to have many responsive and concerned people, like Mr Andrews and the members of International House Council, involved in running the House'.

That there will be an end-of-year House magazine is almost as certain as that there will be an International Night or Candlelight Ceremony. Someone, or some group, makes it happen at the end of almost every year. In the 1980s, it appeared every year except 1982 (when a series of *IH News* newssheets performed many of the same functions) and was predominantly a record of the year's events and personalities. Editions after 1983 are probably more positive in their assessment of House activities than their immediate predecessors, reporting on things that had happened during the year and frequently linking them to the broader context of the House's history and ideals.

In this spirit, the Assistant Editor of the 1987 magazine, Angela Cranston, wrote of that edition: 'The Magazine this year has, in many ways, attempted to be a little bit broader in content than in the past, in trying to reflect not only the interactions within the walls of the House, but also those links with outside interests, whether in Sydney, in Australia, or overseas.' In writing thus, Angela draws attention to a characteristic of the magazines of the eighties, for most were about the experiences of residents in the House in that year, whether informally or as part of the program of activities.

Elizabeth Andrews (seated, left) and Geoffrey Andrews,
with staff and residents, 1989

The magazines of this decade were, then, significantly different from the one of 1968 edited by Elisabeth Hobbs and Richard Waterhouse which contained fourteen essays on matters including student riots in Japan, life in Singapore, two Indonesian poets and the South African policy of Apartheid. That early venture into 'the broader context' was not matched by any comparable publication in the 1980s. This is, no doubt, partly attributable to the comparative youth of residents in the 1980s, but it may also reflect a general retreat in International House resident life, or even Australian university student life, from sustained writing and a desire, instead, to concentrate on the interpersonal experiences of the immediate community.

The positions used to support the IH program of activities varied during the 1980s, largely as the result of funding constraints. In 1980 John Vine was Program Director and Guy Verney and Larry Greentree were Program Assistants; in 1981 Stephen White and Larry Singer were Program Assistants; from 1982 to 1986 I was Deputy Director with responsibility for the program; in 1987 there was no Program Director; and in 1988 Pauline Kennedy returned from a brief retirement to be Assistant Director (Program) until 1993.

During the 1980s the program included a range of items directed to the community outside International House: a splendid series of international concerts organised by Winsome Evans (musician-in-residence, 1980); participation in University Open Days (1980, 1984 and 1988); Alumni Association Foundation Day Addresses from 1981; performances by the All Nations Dance Company from the New York International House (1982); exhibitions by Iraqi and North Korean authorities (1982); orientation programs for overseas scholars of the Australian Universities International Development Program (1984 –1986); a lunchtime series of lectures on themes of international peace and justice (1986); orientation programs for all University of Sydney overseas students (1989); excursions to several NSW schools in connection with their 'Society and Culture' syllabus (1989); and annual recitals by Lauris Elms, the last-mentioned being a cultural event for the benefit of both residents and visitors as well as a fund-raiser.

A good program can induce residents to reflect on the experience of living in the international community of the House, and thereby add rational thought to the unconscious intercultural learning that is facilitated by all the community-building forces in IH. The program can also make use of the wonderful variety of knowledge that exists in an international community and vastly extend a resident's access to knowledge of others' religions, languages, politics, art, geography, history and social institutions. The program can broaden and deepen a resident's knowledge and understanding of their academic field or improve their skills in, say, thesis writing or public speaking. Most importantly, when a number of residents come together in an activity,

The Candlelight Ceremony, 1988

such as an International Night, a bus expedition or a series of talks, they learn the skills of purposive, intercultural co-operation. The key to all these areas of programming is engaging the attention and commitment of House residents. Some activities are organised spontaneously by residents, some by the IHMA and some by a program director. A final area of programming that has received varying degrees of attention during IH's history is the exposure to the wider community of high quality international and intercultural events which are held, even if they attract only very minor attention from current House residents. These involve the House in 'carrying the light' directly into the wider community rather than by the medium of its alumni.

For every year in the 1980s there was an impressive number of program activities, principally, but not solely, for the House's own residents. There were the regular International Nights, Candlelight Ceremonies, Balls, Women's Committee welcome picnics, in-House welcome functions, floor parties and Youth Series orchestral concerts in the Opera House. From 1984 there was the year-opening Flag Ceremony to reflect A. P. Elkin's vision of residents coming from various tribes, each with their own bundle of magic. And then there were the other events, individual or arranged into a series, intellectual or social or sporting. (An extensive list of IH activities throughout the 1980s, appears at the end of this chapter.)

Between 1982 and 1986 the House had its own Rostrum (similar to Toastmasters) organisation. David Walker was the first President. The club met in term time and gave its ten or so members weekly practice in the skills of public speaking. It fostered community development, knowledge of other cultures and skill development. It was the custom of the club to applaud each member when they rose to speak and to applaud them again when they had finished. Overseas and Australian students were involved in roughly equal numbers and a number of faculties were represented. The Club President, Tong Hua, writing in the 1986 magazine, said that as a student from China he had been made President to encourage (successfully) Asian students to join. Attempting to use the magazine as a recruiting medium, he wrote: 'If you feel discontent with the world, come to Rostrum to get a sympathetic audience, because speaking publicly can be your first step of action to change the world; if you feel happy, come to Rostrum to share your happiness with your fellow-residents, because only through sharing can you double your happiness.' The IH club had guest critics from the wider Rostrum fraternity, and hosted a week-long Rostrum convention in 1983. One of the IH club's members, Peter Friend, put his skills to good use in winning, for International House, the inaugural Intercollegiate Oration in 1985 against the representatives of all the University of Sydney colleges and halls of residence. Peter was also a 1986 finalist in the annual NSW Rostrum public speaking competition, representing the International House Club.

Two great facilities for the House program were the bus and the Belanglo Forest Log Cabin. The Log Cabin was used steadily through the first half and probably more intensively through the second half of the decade. It was originally envisaged that pit toilets thirty metres from the Cabin itself and showers from a canvas bag would suffice for those using the cabin and would be a novel and educative bush experience. For many IH residents, however, the addition of such privations to the strangeness of an isolated and eerily silent location was unwelcome. Consistent, enthusiastic use of the cabin would have to wait until these hardships were remedied. The House bus was more consistently used, often travelling interstate for thousands of kilometres on a single trip. In the earlier years of the decade, apart from being used for basic House functions such as provisioning the House shop, the bus was very much a Program facility rather than a private indulgence. Residents were required to have at least three nationalities represented in any excursion group so that the aim of promoting international friendship and understanding could be promoted on any journey. Some residents saw this approach to achieving House aims as unjustifiably heavy-handed and the 1984 survey noted that of those who experienced difficulty in getting the bus, seventeen per cent said it was because they could not find sufficient nationalities.

This statistic comes from a broader survey of the House. In 1983 there was a national study of the needs and wishes of residents of university colleges. In 1984 many of the questions from the national study and some questions of particular relevance to IH residents were combined into a survey which was completed by 158 residents. The survey showed that 84 per cent of respondents were satisfied or very satisfied with the House. A majority of those dissatisfied or very dissatisfied were Australian. The major complaint, as we read in every chapter of this history, was about catering (only 51 per cent satisfied or very satisfied), and a majority of residents wanted to have a say in the appointment of all senior staff. One of the things tested by the survey was residents' assessment of the contributions made to the aims of International House by the residents and administration respectively. The results showed a very positive self-assessment by residents of the extent to which they contributed towards meeting the aims of

International House. Interestingly, they thought they contributed in a better way than the administration.

	Administration				Residents			
	Very well	Well	Poor	Very poor	Very well	Well	Poor	Very poor
Study atmosphere	17	61	17	5	13	61	24	2
Learn of nations	15	64	20	2	26	61	11	2
Friendship and nations	15	56	21	7	27	58	12	3

An important part of IH's interaction with the larger community was through its growing body of alumni. In February 1980 the House Council decided to support the Alumni Association, SUIHAA, by providing part-time secretarial support and by maintaining the alumni address list 'to encourage hard thinking on intercultural and international issues through seminars, contributions to the Newsletter, seminars with students and so on'.

Further, the House constitution was amended to require that Council include at least one alumnus in its membership and procedures were amended to make it more likely that residents would become SUIHAA members when they left the House. 'We hope', read the financial document circulated to residents, 'that when you leave the House you will become a member of the Alumni Association and unless you request otherwise we will transfer from your Key and Breakage Deposit the $10.00 Alumni membership fee'. Thus, quite early in the decade, SUIHAA had become more fully incorporated into the House's formal and financial operations.

In 1981, twenty alumni interested in SUIHAA held a planning meeting to supplement the work that had been done by the House Council. Rosalie McCutcheon (by audio tape) suggested that alumni be host families for current residents, that alumni write for the House magazine, and that there be SUIHAA versus IHMA debates; John Gascoigne and Pali Singh suggested that alumni provide academic guidance and networking opportunities for residents and one another; Rosemary Berrick thought alumni should write about their work for the SUIHAA Newsletter; Brian Farmer suggested arranging talks at International House by internationally significant speakers; Sandy Smith recommended that alumni use the Belanglo Log Cabin; Guy Verney suggested an annual Foundation Day address and an essay competition.

The alumni planning bore immediate fruit. The first Foundation Day Address was delivered by Sir Zelman Cowen, the Governor-General, in August 1981; subsequent addresses were delivered in 1982 by the Honourable Al Grassby (a former immigration minister) and in 1983 by Dr Keith Suter. The 1988 Address was delivered by Dr Walter Westman, a 1967 alumnus who had received the House's Alumni Award for Achievement in 1987 for his work in environmental science and environmental politics. The host family idea went ahead in a limited way during the 1980s; John Gascoigne gave a number of talks to IH residents on thesis writing skills; there were several IHMA versus SUIHAA debates; and alumni did use the Log Cabin and assisted at working bees for its upgrading. The alumni made further contributions to the House's residents by setting up, and donating to, the Rosalie McCutcheon Scholarship and the Graeme de Graaff Scholarship.

By 1980, the SUIHAA Newsletter had progressed from basic roneoed sheets to an offset-printed publication. The print was small and the layout was literally 'cut and paste', undertaken by some of the alumni, but it did have photographs and the small print and thin paper enabled printing and postage costs to be minimised. By the end of the decade, the Newsletter was showing all the benefits of improved technology and increased funding in its typesetting, printing and more numerous photographs. Newsletters of the early eighties concentrated on keeping alumni up to date on one another's movements and activities, but those appearing towards the end of the decade acted more as a showcase for the House itself. The November 1989 edition, for example, devoted the first five of its fourteen pages to the Director's comments about the House, its history and recent developments; three pages were devoted to news of alumni; there was an article about the contribution of IH residents to 'Studies in Society and Culture' courses in several NSW schools; and there was an article by SUIHAA Chairperson, Greg Bird, on the continuing relevance to alumni of their IH experience. The Newsletters also included a written argument between three alumni about attitudes to conservation, spread over two editions in 1988, and an article by Joan Rowlands about her experience of teaching English in China in that same year.

It is an endearing, if frustrating, characteristic of the Alumni Newsletter that until the late eighties the Newsletter editor and the SUIHAA President and committee members were so modest that it is almost impossible to ascertain all their names from the Newsletter. Throughout the decade, SUIHAA continued to develop roles for itself as: a club to maintain convivial contact between its members; a promoter of international knowledge and understanding; and a source of support for the House and its residents.

In all of these areas SUIHAA exhibited innovation and achievement during the decade. The Foundation Day Addresses, in particular, were a contribution to the 1980 House Council's desire for 'hard thinking on intercultural and international issues through seminars, contributions to the Newsletter, seminars with students and so on'. What was beginning to become visible was the possibility of a body which would make each group of residents see themselves as the newest members of a fellowship that supported, encouraged and challenged them to achieve what the most successful of their older brothers and sisters had achieved for international goodwill.

Within the House, residents continued to benefit from community support and particularly from IH's traditional volunteer supporters, for the most part associated with, if not recruited by, the Women's Committee. The Committee not only paid for material improvements for the House and the Log Cabin but additionally contributed to the needs of the residents directly with many thousands of dollars in bursaries for impecunious residents and an annual 'welcome picnic' at the home of one of its members. Olga and Les Kemp, for example, opened their Avalon seaside home to a coach full of residents on a number of occasions for this picnic. The Committee's money-raising activities included not only the wonderful Lauris Elms concerts already mentioned, but, Melbourne Cup luncheons, fashion parades, a Festival of the Four Winds and guest speaker events. The long-serving Convenor of the Women's Committee, Kathleen O'Neil, also used to augment the funds by selling her homemade jams and pickles at meetings of the Committee.

Associated with the Women's Committee were Una Henderson and Gay Fisher, who continued to work in the House library throughout the decade; Mollie Burns, who devoted hundreds of hours to the House's gardens; Valda Lyle, who assisted with planning for the visit of the All Nations Dance Company in 1982; and Betty Boulton, who discovered the House at the 1984 University Open Day and, being lonely in Sydney after arriving from the country, was happy to help such a worthwhile institution to prosper. Rosemary Berrick, the volunteer archivist from the 1970s, continued to take photographs of any function she attended, to collect photographs of any she did not attend and conscientiously to paste into books the photographs and administrative records which make much of the history of those decades engaging and accessible.

From 1984, Sylvia Hellyer for several years arranged visits to Sydney homes and country areas for IH overseas students who wanted to meet Australians in their homes; many were introduced to Australian families through their friendship with Australian IH residents, but many were not, and Sylvia Hellyer's work was a benefit to them.

Most of the members of the Women's Committee were the wives of University of Sydney academics, who saw International House as a prestigious, socially enlightened and interesting institution which they were pleased to be involved in supporting. In addition to providing homely comforts, they had a degree of quasi-maternal communication with residents through the House shop and home hospitality. By the eighties, however, some of the original committee members had died or progressed beyond the point of energetic fund-raising. The young women who, in a static society, might have replaced them, were instead pursuing careers of their own and therefore lacked the time and inclination to join such an enterprise. The Women's Committee relinquished control of the IH shop to the IHMA in 1980, thereby losing one regular point of contact with residents and Sylvia Hellyer's initiative came to a halt before the end of the decade. Nevertheless, the Committee was then still in a very active mode and undertook about a dozen fund-raising activities in 1989.

The Women's Committee was the main source of bursaries in the 1980s, but bursary funds were also contributed by the Soroptomists charitable group, a Country Women's Association group, and the families of the late Harold Maze and the late Michael Rathgeber. Rotary also continued its involvement with the House. Former Rotary District Governor Ian Hudson remained on the Council and donated generously to a range of appeals. The Rotary Club of Newtown continued to contribute to the House library on an annual basis and one of its members, Basil Voyagis, was a member of Council for most of the decade (and later Chair). Program Directors had reason to be grateful to Rotary clubs also, as the Gosford West, Gladesville, Chatswood, Hornsby, Blacktown, Mosman, Parramatta, St Ives and Lake Cargelligo clubs provided hospitality to IH residents.

There were some striking events in the 1980s. The great fire of 1984 was one. Assistant Director Julia Arnold found herself early on an August Sunday morning confronted by a Wool Room dense with smoke and a fire burning in one of the upstairs television rooms. The fire brigade managed to extinguish the fire but there was $29,000 worth of damage to the television rooms, the meditation room, the Wool Room and furniture and furnishings. The fire, the rapidity of its spread, the extent of the damage and the recognition that there was only one stairway to escape from the top-level rooms in an emergency, ensured

Diane and Howard Cook, Doreen Langley and Molly Maze,
the opening of the Maze Building, 1985

that safety aspects of the Rotunda building would be subjected to further scrutiny in the years ahead.

The opening of the Maze Building was another major event and involved a visit of the former President of the New York International House, Howard Cook, to open the new building in November 1985. The Maze Building was a new concept for IH. It was designed as a group of apartments overlooking the quadrangle formed by itself, the original North Wing, the East Wing and the Elkin Wing. It provided a new option in accommodation because the apartments were larger than existing accommodation in the House and they were all self-catering. The furniture was chosen to be domestic rather than institutional, with the aim of ensuring that each unit had a homely ambience. The House's experience with one child, Sawali, who had lived in the flat on level 1 of the North Wing with her parents Dinesh and Swate Sarvate in the mid-eighties, and the popularity of occasional child visitors to the House produced a general confidence that children in the Maze Building would be a welcome addition to the population of the enlarged House.

The Maze Building had the great advantage that it enabled International House to determine, subject to University approval, what would be built facing City Road, immediately to the south of its original dormitory wing. The question about the Maze Building, however, was whether its residents would become part of the larger IH community or whether, having their own dining facilities, they would lack the desire to mix. If the new facilities were to encourage a greater variety of persons to join International House, the Maze Building could enhance the House's social and intellectual environment. But if the new arrivals simply kept to themselves, they might set an example of disengagement that could even spread to the dormitory buildings. If that happened, the Maze residents would contribute to the House's economies of scale but could otherwise be a negative influence.

In the first years of the Maze Building's existence there was some beneficial mixing, promoted by the entry of some interesting residents, including children, and by the inclusion in the Maze residents' contracts of a number of meals in the dining room free of charge. The IHMA Chairman, Vishwanath Ramakrishnan, wrote at the end of 1986 that 'the residents of the Maze Building were successfully integrated into mainstream of the house'. The 1986 magazine substantiates his claim with its story on a family of early Maze residents, Robert and Anna Dole and their son, Patrick, from Quebec. The Doles participated in the Table Française language group and contributed young Patrick to International Night variously as a sheep in the Australian act, as a sandwich-board holder in the American act and in a number of other minor roles.

Another prominent early Maze resident was the extraordinary septuagenarian, Professor Arthur Goodfriend, veteran journalist, diplomat, academic and Peace Corps worker. Arthur, who had come into contact with Hitler, Mussolini, Gandhi, Stalin and Emperor Hirohito in his long and adventurous life, gave a talk to residents. He also made whimsical watercolour sketches of things he had enjoyed while in Australia and, by way of compensation for having blue-tacked them to every square metre of wall in his Maze unit, gave them to the House when he departed. Framed, they hung on the wall of what was then known as the Coffee Shop for many years until replaced by a collection of photographs after some residents, who thought some of Arthur's pictures 'culturally insensitive', requested their removal. It was his practice to keep a journal, a practice that he said ensured he would not lead a dull life. His memoirs are reportedly stored in the University of Hawaii's Hamilton Library.

The ideals of IH, University of Sydney, continued to be maintained and renewed by contact with the larger International House movement around the world. During the 1980s, there were several occasions on which the House furthered communication with its progenitors. In 1983 I undertook a three-month study tour of forty International Houses,

Centres and offices in the USA, working briefly in two of the Houses and studying the programs developed in the other Houses and Centres; in 1985 Graeme de Graaff attended the meeting of the heads of the major International Houses in New York; Geoffrey Andrews hosted the February 1988 meeting of the Heads of International Houses in Sydney. And later that year Geoffrey undertook a study tour of the Berkeley, Chicago, Philadelphia, New York and London Houses. Those who had gone on study tours found them a source of inspiration. The programs of activities in 1984, 1985 and 1986 owe a great deal to the ideas gained in my 1983 tour; Graeme de Graaff said that he came back from his 1985 trip 'with batteries recharged'; and Geoffrey Andrews appears to have drawn on his trip and the 1988 Sydney meeting for much of the thought and inspiration in his 1989 paper, 'The Future for International House'. Reports on each of the trips and meetings are included in the minutes of Council.

The major event involving the overseas International Houses was certainly Sydney's hosting of the 1988 meeting. This had been set up by Graeme de Graaff during his 1985 visit to the USA. When the conference was held, it involved directors from the Brisbane, Chicago, Melbourne, New York, Tokyo, University of New South Wales, Osaka, Paris, Philadelphia and Wollongong Houses staying in the Sydney IH, discussing matters such as: management, orientation and resident well-being, academic and program responsibilities, development and alumni affairs, board-staff relationships, foreign relations, outreach and public relations, role of students in operations, and the relationship between a House and a university. The conference received a letter of welcome from the Prime Minister and enjoyed a reception by the Governor-General, Sir Ninian Stephen, in his official Sydney residence.

Throughout the decade, there was a good deal of concern to plan the future of the House. In October 1979 the IH Council had resolved 'that a small committee with wide terms of reference should be established to review and make recommendations concerning the fabric, purpose and administration of the House for the 1980s', and that 'submissions should be encouraged from all interested people and parties'. Questions designed to stimulate relevant comment were sent to members of Council, selected members of SUIHAA, the IHMA, other International Houses and the Australian Development Assistance Bureau (ADAB). Nineteen written and verbal submissions were received in response to 56 requests.

The resulting 'Report of the 1980s' Committee' was finalised in January 1980 and highlighted both the good and the bad news:

- the House's existing population comprised at least as many postgraduates as undergraduates, two-and-a-half times as many men as women, residents from 26 countries and approximately equal numbers of overseas and Australian students;
- the Government policy of encouraging overseas students to study in Australian universities had just come to a sudden end, but the prestige of the University of Sydney and the relatively small size of its overseas student body would probably ensure that International House was little affected;
- the Alumni Association required strengthening 'to promote the exchange of international ideas, knowledge and cultures';
- International House was little known throughout the University;
- all but one submission had advocated the House remaining at its present size to maintain its 'atmosphere';
- all submissions referred to the House as having an outstanding Director;
- the ideal IH Council member brings to the House expertise in a particular field and encourages the Director to use that expertise in the interests of the House;
- the appointment of a full-time Assistant Director could release some pressure on the Director, Bursar and House secretary;
- apart from the tenth anniversary celebrations, there had been 'little to show the world that we are an International House';
- apart from the initial Rotary fund-raising campaign which had allowed the original building to be built, a meagre $50,000 had been raised from private sources.

The committee's most significant recommendations were as follows:

- Enhance the House's publicity material to attract more women, especially Australian women, to International House and to bring its population mix to half overseas–half Australian, half men–half women, and at least half postgraduate.
- Discontinue non-resident membership of International House, which seemed to be achieving little, if anything, that was worthwhile.
- Support future growth of the Alumni Association by providing part-time secretarial support and the maintenance of up-to-date contact lists to encourage 'hard thinking on intercultural and international issues through seminars, contributions to the Newsletter, seminars with students and so on'.

- Ensure that at least one member of IH Council is an alumnus.
- Give each student an opportunity to invite a University staff member to a meal at IH without charge.
- Develop plans for Stage 4 of International House, a high rise building with apartment units, a squash court, a gymnasium and seminar rooms and a central courtyard with a swimming pool. Stage 4 to be completed in the 1980s.
- Define the procedure for the selection of a Director, including the composition of a selection committee including the Vice-Chancellor, the IHMA Chairman and the alumnus member of Council.
- Amend the IH constitution to require that the Council include an alumnus, a second member of the IHMA, the Assistant Director and a Fellow of the University Senate who is not a University administrative staff member.
- Write to each Council member at the end of his term of appointment asking him to indicate in writing whether he has the necessary time to continue as a member.
- Create the International House membership of 'Fellow', to honour those who have served the House, as a member of Council or otherwise.
- Restrict the chairmanship of Council and House and Finance Committee to two-year terms.
- Appoint a full-time Assistant Director to relieve the pressures on the Director, Bursar and House secretary.

The committee and its report appear to have been driven by Doreen Langley, with the agreement of the Director. One of its goals was to re-invigorate the membership of the Council, as well as providing recognition of those who served on Council by creating the honour 'Fellow of International House'.

The committee also wanted approval for Stage 4 to go ahead, notwithstanding the concern of many respondents to resist an increase in size that might threaten the 'atmosphere' of the House. There had been opposition to each of the previous extensions, the East Wing and the Elkin Wing, on the same grounds, so it was prudent to assess the nature, location and strength of such potential opposition to Stage 4. Finally, they wanted to strengthen the Alumni Association, reduce the role of the University in the administration of the House, increase the number of female residents, provide additional administrative support to the Director and tidy up any loose ends.

In considering the work of this committee, it is also instructive to focus on what it was *not* concerned about and did *not* want to change. The IHMA, for example, was mentioned only to the extent that it should have more representation on the Council. The psycho-social quality of the House was referred to only by reference to the desire to *maintain* the 'atmosphere'. The caterers were not mentioned, evidently because this was one of the few occasions in the history of the House when the catering was highly regarded. Concern with the particular needs of overseas students was shown only to the extent of proposing that they enhance their communication (and the House's) with the University community by each year inviting a University staff member to lunch as a guest. The House's international program scored no recommendations but was mentioned in three places: in reference to the lack of achievement since the tenth Anniversary celebrations; in the expression of hope that the Alumni Association would 'promote the exchange of international ideas, knowledge and cultures' and 'encourage hard thinking'; and in a reference to the great effectiveness of temporary Program Directors and student Program Assistants.

The 'Report of the 1980s Committee' was the report of a body fundamentally happy with the House and its achievements. Its members were aware of the way in which the House had twice extended beyond its initial size of 120, with the addition of the East and Elkin wings, to a population of 190 and, though the Elkin Wing had only been open a few months, they were not apprehensive about any consequent damage to the House's 'atmosphere'. The committee members were now moving with vigour, confidence and politic sensitivity towards further achievements.

The Council meeting of February 1980 adopted the report with relatively minor amendments. A tennis court was substituted for the swimming pool and the gymnasium became a gymnasium/badminton court. Significantly, however, the committee's detailed procedures for the appointment of a Director were set aside in favour of consultation between Professor Michael Taylor (Deputy Vice-Chancellor and a Fellow of Senate as well as a member of Council) and the Vice-Chancellor, Professor Bruce Williams. The proposal that the Council include a Fellow of Senate who was not a University administrative staff member was likewise unsuccessful. The University administration had gently asserted its influence over the House.

The plan to create fellowships of International House received the approval of the University Senate and went ahead in 1980. Founding members of Council, Sir Bernard Freeman, Mr Harold Maze, Dr

Geoffrey Howe and Sir Harold Wyndham were made Fellows of International House, as were the University Chancellor, Sir Herman Black, Mrs Rosalie McCutcheon and the founding members of the Women's Committee, Mrs Kathleen O'Neil and Mrs Thelma Bate. The existing members remained on Council, except Brian Farmer who, in accordance with his view of such matters, worked furiously and skilfully for a number of years and then resigned so that someone else could take up the running.

The eighties saw the end of the de Graaff years for International House: Pauline Kennedy left her full-time position at the House to have a family in November 1984, Rosalie McCutcheon performed her last formal service for the House with a speech to the 1985 final House Dinner; and Graeme de Graaff retired on 6 March 1987. All, it must be said, left at the peak of their powers. The challenge was to find people equally good to put in their place. Pauline's contribution to International House has been commented on in earlier chapters. Her energy, loyalty and ebullient goodwill continued in the 1980s and to it she added confidence and authority. The sense that International House was a place of humane efficiency was established for visitors before they left the reception area, and for residents it was reinforced each time they went out from, or returned to, the House. It was more demanding for the rest of us when she left, because the biggest engine of goodwill was missing. Graeme ran his own engine at higher revs to make up the shortfall. It was a fine piece of work by the Director that led to her being re-recruited a few years later to be part-time alumni co-ordinator and, later again, part-time Assistant Director (program).

A farewell dinner was held for Graeme de Graaff at International House on Friday evening, 6 March 1987. The May SUIHAA Newsletter reported that the function was a memorable one, attracting alumni from far and wide, including many who had not been seen in International House for years. Brian Farmer gave the keynote address, recounting the founding Director's achievements over 22 years and broadcasting a phone call from Rosalie McCutcheon in Adelaide to the assembled diners. There are written records of a number of Alumni who, though unable to attend, wanted their greetings and recollections to be conveyed to the gathering. They expressed gratitude for Graeme's insightful and painstaking attention to their individual needs and the way he had made the House such an educational success. Walter Westman spoke of IH being 'like a grand salon, a place of culture and the lively arts where people felt free to try out new ideas and pursue political ideals within an environment that would welcome them unconditionally'. Ros Wood said he had 'gently pushed' on her the idea that peace is possible because we can live with one another's differences, not just because we are in some ways 'the same underneath'. In the messages of Mitsuyoshi Adachi, Tan Seng Huat, Tony Chiu, Howard Clark, Sofronio San Juan, Atsuko Kouda, Fani Nicolaidis, Betty Nance-Smith, Dinesh Sarvate and Peter Chin ran words like: 'dignified', 'kind heart', 'help and counsel', 'kind adviser', 'bring out the best', 'a man for all seasons', 'wise counsellor', 'welcome smile and warmth', 'guiding hand' and 'simply the perfect'. Andrew Loewenthal, a 1967 alumnus who was a member of Council in the mid-eighties, told me at that time that he thought Graeme was always several moves ahead of the game, seeing more and seeing, earlier than the rest of us, opportunities for International House to do good, for the individuals associated with it and for the wider community. People close to decision-making in International House over a long period realised that most of the House's advances were achieved after Graeme had planted the seed of one of his ideas in the mind of a likely champion and then supported its gestation and growth. I can recall Harold Maze, a penetrating judge of such matters, expressing delight at the way that he made it all look easy.

Mrs Mac's final speech to a House Dinner came at the end of a few days' stay in 1985. At the end of that year there were, as always, plenty of thoughtful and good-hearted people about with a happy and successful year behind them, but there was cynicism as well, and a much younger and larger population than had heard serious House Dinner speeches in the 1960s. Mrs Mac was the heavy artillery of International House spirituality. But she was old, she was barely audible and her voice quavered. She could make subtle truths about the multicultural human condition widely accessible but, in the IH dining room and the context of an end-of-year dinner, would the residents listen? The room was silent through her twenty-minute speech. I recall a sense of awe in the unsolicited comments of several residents after the dinner. It was clear that her vision had reached a receptive audience.

Rosalie McCutcheon, like Pauline Kennedy, attributed much of the success of her IH-related work to Graeme de Graaff. Rosalie's biographer quotes from a letter she wrote to Graeme in 1987:

> This morning I was thinking about my three great Bosses
> — Margaret Holmes, Winifred West and G de G and,
> strangely, I could formulate only the words — to love,
> honour and obey (!!) within an ambience (is that the word)
> of complete freedom and personal growth. M.H. and W.W.
> were older women; you were a younger man and I was

62. I still marvel at it. With you I began the first day of the
rest of my life, a life that continues to surprise me and my
friends, a life full of discovery. In a sense nothing surprises
me — and: everything surprises me.

Those acquainted with Rosalie McCutcheon will recognise in this
fragment of a personal letter the humility, the openness to unfamiliar
ideas, the sense of wonder and joy, the loyalty, the instinct to commitment, the sincerity and the ability to express very personal ideas that had
made her such a potent influence on the culture of International House.

Graeme de Graaff's successor, Geoffrey Andrews, came to
International House after a period as Headmaster of The Armidale
School. He had had several years' introduction to International House,
however, through his son, Richard, who had been IHMA Chairman
in 1985 and who had taken some of his fellow residents to meet his
family. Geoffrey's first Council meeting as Director was on 19 March
1987. The Chairman of Council was George Lean, formerly the Chief
Executive of the huge Peko Wallsend Mining Company and a generous
benefactor of the House. The minutes of the meeting record that Lean
asked Council members to stand to welcome the new Director and
then raised some issues about the long-term nature and direction of the
House. He had asked the retiring Director to prepare an assessment of
the House as he was leaving it and read part of this. George Lean then
quoted the objectives of International House:

- to provide an educational environment for Australian and overseas
  students of the University with provision for both residents and
  non-resident students and such others as may assist its purposes;
- to promote greater understanding and fellowship between people
  of different nationalities by education and other suitable means;
- to promote the ideal of International House, 'That brotherhood
  may prevail';
- to promote the exchange of international ideas, knowledge and
  cultures;
- to provide tutorial services to resident and non-resident students
  in their preparation for their university studies and examinations.

The Chairman's response to such ideals was to say:

As I contemplate these objectives I find them almost
oppressive. This is just my own personal reaction and my
thoughts to Council are, whether this year we should give
some sort of assessment as to the direction in which we
are going. I would be very depressed if in three years time

Mr Andrews was to say he does not enjoy running and operating the House.

When the Chairman asked for comments, Sir Harold Wyndham suggested that the Director might structure a committee to report to Council in about nine months and Doreen Langley enquired whether the new Director had ideas he would like to discuss. Geoffrey Andrews nominated two matters of concern: the role of the House Council and the necessity 'to show the world that international living and co-operation, as witnessed by International House, can occur other than in a hot-house atmosphere'. The meeting accepted the Director's suggestion that the July meeting of Council should be a seminar on the role of Council and the future direction of the House.

Inevitably, the arrival of a new Director brought change in its wake. On assuming office he set in train a re-evaluation of the role of the House and its place within the University and the larger community. In particular, he thought that issues such as the image of the House, fund-raising and contacts with groups such as Rotary and Chambers of Commerce should be reviewed.

The new Director's goal of renewing and extending bridges between the House and the wider community of international students became more evident as he settled into the post. It was evident, for example, in his statement in the May 1987 SUIHAA Newsletter that 'ways must be found to show that this experiment in international understanding works not only in the microcosm of the House, but also in the widest global sphere'. To achieve such ends, the new Director proposed the construction of a program and overseas student administrative centre so that International House would become the centre for overseas students at the University while maintaining its vital links with Australian students.

As noted in the preceding chapter, International House had experimented in the early seventies with sharing the House's resident facilities with a large non-resident population and found the benefits outweighed by the damage to the resident experience. Here was the idea surfacing again, with modifications to be sure, but also with significant similarities. As the next chapter on the 1990s outlines, once again, as in the 1970s, the issue of the wider reach of IH beyond the immediate needs of the residents was to prompt a mixture of idealism, hard work, mixed success and disappointment.

Council's response to the Director's paper of May 1989 was to create a Sub-Committee Looking into Possible Future Directions of the House, chaired by the new Chairman of Council, Professor Hans Freeman.

By the time of the sub-committee's second report in October 1989, the possible further extension of International House was to be kept 'under review' and discussion was concentrating on how to improve the existing facilities and operations. The sub-committee reported on the desirability of:

- Improvement to lighting and other facilities in study bedrooms and corridors;
- Extending the foyer by removing the shop and storeroom;
- Improvement to the garden, roof and courtyard;
- Promoting IH as a forum for distinguished speakers from Australia and overseas;
- Introducing a program of resident scholars and artists;
- Making the Wool Room and dining room more accessible to non-residents;
- Preventing noise from the Rotunda gallery from disturbing functions in the Wool Room;
- Improving such Wool Room facilities as projection, stage, storage and lighting;
- Modifying the dining room to make the garden more accessible;
- Providing new common rooms on Floors 4–8 of the North Wing.

Overall, the eighties was a period that built on the consolidation and measured progress of the seventies. The decade started out with great confidence and with a desire by the most energetic members of Council for further evolutionary development: a final building that would cover the available real estate and provide a new type of accommodation for a new type of resident; increased programming, administrative and alumni resources; and increased representation in the House's governing bodies for staff, students and alumni.

Many of the aspirations of the Council for the eighties were met, but during the decade the ground on which these aspirations had been built moved. By 1985, with the looming end to government financial assistance to halls of residence, with the University applying user-pays principles even to its internal clients, and with the change from terms to semesters undermining the potential for vacation conference income, the funding situation looked doubtful. Towards the end of the decade, however, the House's finances again became secure as it was evident that large numbers of full-fee-paying overseas students could be expected in the 1990s. The overseas student boom, in turn, would drive a significant demographic change: many of these full-fee-paying overseas students would be undergraduates and, therefore, in search of supervised accommodation; and along with the long-term overseas students would come a growing number of undergraduate students, especially from the USA, on single semester exchanges, wanting to internationalise their degree by incorporating in it a semester at an exchange university such as Sydney. The demographic change would, in turn, lead to an increase in the expectations of students with respect to such matters as telephone connections, air conditioning and bathroom facilities, matters which had barely rated a mention in the resident survey held as recently as 1984.

Physically, the House developed by the completion of its natural building area, but no sooner had this been done than the need for renovation and improvement began to become pressing. Socially, the House gained families and some more senior residents by the addition of the Maze Building. The proportion of women increased in International House, as it did in the student population generally, so that by the end of the decade there were practically equal numbers of women and men. The number of Australian postgraduate women residents had fallen to zero, however, and the proportion of Australian residents generally fell to below 40 per cent. International House could clearly survive as a self-funding entity, but could it maintain, and even extend, the ideals with which it had been founded? Such were the issues with which the Council and the Director had to grapple as the eighties gave way to a new decade.

House activities during the 1980s

The following extensive, but by no means complete, list has been gleaned from a variety of House magazines and reports. The number of entries for each year reflects to some extent the ready availability of source material:

1980

Miss International House Quest (satirical)

Bad Taste Party

Pyjama Party

Corroboree

The Alternative Games

Music Committee recitals and variety evening

Japanese, Indonesian, Hong Kong and Indian nights

Coffee Shop seminars organised by Guy Verney on: saltwater crocodiles in

Northern Australia; readings in Australian poetry and literature; the art and architecture of Venice, Munich, Florence and Rome; high fibre diets; energy; the anthropology of food in South-east Asia; the United Nations and the law of the sea; Australia's relations with Asia; solar energy and architecture; understanding the modern guerrilla: the Eritrean Liberation Army (film); the future of South-east Asia; natural pollution in northern NSW; cultural nationalism in Canada and South Africa; Buddhism and Nepal

Weekend seminar on Southern Africa

Residents attended meetings of the Australian Institute of International Affairs

The Australian Institute of Political Science, the Australia/China Education Society, and the Humanist Society of Australia held seminars

Cairns bus trip

Piano recital by Neil Semmler, student at the Conservatorium

National Lieder Society of Australia recital

Scientific films supplied by the Australian & New Zealand Association for the Advancement of Science

Sport: Regular groups for soccer, badminton, squash, tennis, snooker, table tennis, touch football

1981

Musician-in-Residence series of musical events

Inaugural Foundation Day Address by Sir Zelman Cowen

First annual IHMA–SUIHAA Debate (Joan Rowlands, Chair)

Program of talks, informal sports, excursions and films arranged by the Assistant Directors

Sport: IH Soccer team in the men's college competition

1982

Series of film evenings featuring classic films

Guest speakers: Mark Foong on love; Shirley Haight on the U.S. and the third world; Dr Debesh Bhattacharya on trade between developed and developing countries; Peter Valder on curious and diverse flora of Australia

Cooking demonstrations by Andy Tse, Deedy Kalangie and Hari Murthi

Visits to Rotary Club of Blacktown

Excursion to NSW Parliament, as guest of the Hon. Franca Arena

Seymour Centre productions using free tickets

National nights of Fiji and Hong Kong

Bible study group and 'Poet's Corner group'

Debate organised by John Spurlock: 'To preserve peace, first prepare for war'

Foundation Day Address by the Hon. Al Grassby on multiculturalism

Ferry cruise and visit to Old Sydney Town

Sport: cricket, volleyball and tennis

1983

Greek films, organised by Stilianos Rafailidis

In-House Insight series by residents on their fields of interest: Jimmy Chua on civil engineering and the building industry; Marty Finnemore on politics in the USA; Gillian Pollack on medieval French literature; Andy Tse on town planning

Guest speakers: Dr Henri Rathgeber, 'What is science and where is it going?'; Dr Pollak on pesticides and the environment; Professor Eric Sharpe, 'What is religion?'; Professor Kamiya on Japan's security and the environment; Dr Herbison-Evans on Computers and dance; Anthony Brooke on nuclear disarmament; Professor Moore on astrology and quantum mechanics; Professor Arony on racism and human rights in Australia; Dr John Cheung on ideas for mathematics teaching; Dr Van Langenberg, 'Mystics, Modernisers and Magnates in Indonesia; Dr Keith Suter, 'How will World War III break out?'; Mr J Martin, 'What the Student Committee for Overseas Students can do for you'; Dr J Ward, 'Why a medical association for the prevention of war?'; Senator Colin Mason on Timor; Professor Fan, 'Science, technology and education in modern China'; Dr J Alonso, 'Recent advances in process control computers'

Harbour Bridge fun run

International House car rally

Easter Show outing

Picnic and port inspection tour

Walk Against Want

Peace workshop by guest speaker, Eva Pinthus

Visit to Gladesville Rotary Club

Lake Eyre, illustrated talk by John and Roma Dulhunty

Variety night

40-Hour fast

Centre for Asian Studies talk: 'The search for truth and beauty'

Foundation Day Address: Dr Keith Suter on World War III

Warren Centre talk, Professor Sir Bruce Williams: 'Technical change in a time of depression'

IHMA–SUIHAA debate: 'That big brother is watching you'

Aboriginal dance group performance

Sport: table tennis competition, volleyball competition, tennis competition and swimming carnival

1984

Coffee night, featuring food, coffee, wine

Ideas nights, guest speakers on: cancer research, foreign aid, development economics, Australian foreign policy, postgraduate study

Belgian Consul General, film evening

IHMA Library Committee

Activities Market to showcase pre-programmed activities in the House

Indonesian conversation class

Ballroom dancing (teacher, Nell Challingworth)

Bible study group

Conversation groups: Japanese (with Kaori Okano), Indonesian (with Bernadetha Sarono), Cantonese and English

Computer use group

Painting workshop

Aboriginal institutions in Sydney

International folksong group

Women's Committee: Festival of the Four Winds

Sport: swimming, table tennis, tennis, badminton, squash, volleyball, soccer, snooker, fun run, Thai boxing and inter-floor fun run

Inaugural soccer and volleyball matches against IH UNSW

1985

Variety Night

Ideas nights, guest speakers on: family, sexuality, alternative lifestyles, arms limitation, Christianity, science in the Soviet Union, education in China, Apartheid, the Red Cross blood transfusion service, new areas in biochemistry, exploring Lake Eyre, Buddhism, international law, discrimination law, coping with postgraduate research, air pollution, persecution and repression of minorities, equal opportunity, sexual harassment

Residents' talks on Easter and writing epic legends

Series of talks organised by Will Barton, featuring the representatives of various anti-nuclear professional groups: doctors, nurses, scientists, etc

Series of talks on nuclear armaments, leading to a Model United Nations Security Council

Series of lectures by Dr A Sharma on Hinduism, convened by Papavinasasundaram

Perspectives on Life and Living, convened by Chris Wade and Simon Swinson

Australian Institute of International Affairs, symposium on Australia's defence

Visit to Hurlstone Agricultural High School

Corroboree

Mandarin conversation group, initiated by Wendy Chang

French conversation group

Ballroom dancing classes

The Wasps, play

Women's Committee: Festival of the Four Winds; guest speaker on Bass Strait oil rigs

Blood donations and support for the 40-Hour Famine and Salvation Army Red Shield Appeal

Sport: inter-floor swimming and volleyball competitions; table tennis, badminton, tennis, squash, aerobics, hockey, soccer

1986

Welcome party

Harbour cruise

Workshops introducing Australian history, geography, and culture

Speciality House dinner, addressed by spokespersons for many academic and non-academic services in the University

Model United Nations Security Council

IH and Staff–Student Committee for the Introduction of Peace Studies: Peace Studies Workshop

World Education Fellowship, address by Dr Keith Suter

International Year of Peace, lunchtime addresses: 'Aspects of Peace and Justice: Peace and Justice, Are they Related?'; 'The Earth, its Productivity and Limits'; 'A US Perspective on Peace and Justice'; 'A USSR Perspective on Peace and Justice'

H.V. Evatt Memorial Foundation conference on Australia and the Pacific

Series of talks on relations between the sexes

Series of talks on the law, society, crime and punishment with: Greg James, QC; Hon. Terry Sheahan, NSW Attorney-General, on drugs and the law; Gerry Hay, Department of Corrective Services, on the theory and practice of the prison system in NSW; all of the foregoing inspired by the Barlow and Chambers drug case in Malaysia

Series of American Fulbright scholars' talks on: education and economic development; Gorbachev's first year; and the legal position of women in the USA

Series of talks on Aboriginal themes: peace, intercultural communication and Redfern; Aboriginal health in the Northern Territory; and Aboriginal land rights

The Shadow Minister for Education in NSW on his portfolio and the role of the Member of Parliament in the planning process

Miscellaneous guest speakers on: nuclear winter theory; intellectual suppression; New Zealand after ANZUS; genetics, bacteriology, and creative physics; the position of women in Islam

Visits to a Hindu temple and the Great Synagogue

Songkran and Chinese Moon Festival celebrations

French and Japanese conversation groups

Language lessons in Japanese, Indonesian and Italian given by residents

Ballroom dancing

Poetry reading gatherings for TEFL students and others

Visits to Australian homes in city and country

Visits to: historic sites, Halley's Comet-watching expedition, Railway Museum at Thirlmere, the ANZAC Day march in the city, Sydney Stock Exchange, Royal Easter Show, Luna Park

Visits to Rotary Club of Gosford West, Rotary Club of Eastwood

Corroboree for residents of Sydney and Melbourne International Houses, held in Melbourne.

Sport: soccer, tennis, volleyball, squash, badminton, basketball, cricket

1987

Ballroom dancing

IH played host to a group of deaf children and their mothers

Corroboree at IH Sydney

Australia's Wonderland excursion

Guest speaker: The Hon. Al Grassby on multiculturalism

Harbour cruise

Songkran Festival celebration

Japan Day, featuring panel exhibition, performance of traditional Japanese dance, traditional Japanese toy games, tea ceremony, Judo demonstration, film show, Japanese lunch

Sport: soccer, badminton

1988

Video nights

Coffee nights

Centennial Park picnic

The Oz trip

Hunter Valley trip

Harbour cruise

Bush dance

An IH Cultural Forum, including 'Faces of Buddha'

Corroboree trip to Brisbane

Guest speakers: Scientists Against Nuclear Arms

Sport; IH representative teams in Frisbee (organiser Ann Reekie), softball (led by Mike Cloonan), volleyball (co-ordinator, PH Phongsavan); IH swimming carnival

1989

Evening visits to Gosford and Balmoral Rotary Clubs

Holiday visit to Lake Cargelligo Rotary Club

Visits to the homes of Council members Doreen Langley and Brian Farmer

Visit to NSW Parliament

Speakers: The Hon. Franca Arena on multiculturalism; John Gascoigne on postgraduate study; Helen Sham-Ho on being an Asian member of the NSW Parliament; Paolo Totaro on racism; Nick Stuart on being a correspondent in China during the student revolt; Anne Gray on Aboriginal issues; Annie Andrews on study planning and coping with stress; Mary Wilson on studying and working in China

National day meals provided by the House caterer for Iraq, India, Malaysia, Indonesia, Spain, Greece, Korea, China, Greece, Italy

Indian dance event

Excursion to Lithgow to assist with a workshop for senior school students taking the course 'Society and Culture'

Excursion to Gunnedah for more 'Society and Culture' activities

Japanese tea ceremony

Chinese Moon Festival event

Visit for a spit roast by recently departed former residents

The Committee for Fun: cocktail parties, coffee nights, horror nights, Sale of the Century, beach party, luau followed by a '60s and 70s Get Down, Get Funky' disco

Australia's Wonderland visit

Harbour cruise

Hunter Valley excursion

Bake a cake competition

Belanglo Forest and historic Berrima walks

Sport: Aussie Rules, softball

Sporting excursions to: ice skating, bowling, horse-riding

Sources

University of Sydney Archives:
Council minutes and related papers for the period 1980–1989 (G85/1)
IH House magazines
SUIHAA Newsletters

IH archives:
Material relevant to this chapter is to be found as follows:
1. General: Box 2 File 1.4, Scrapbook; Box 4, File 1.15, IH Director's Report; Box 5, 1.20, 'Report of 1980s Committee', Roger Wescombe's Study Tour; Box 5, File 1.23, Proceedings of international meeting of IH heads, University of Sydney, 1988
2. Events: Box 1, File 3.2, House Dinners 1980s; Box 2, file 3.19, International Peace and Justice talks
3. Residents and members: Box 1, File 7.6, Minutes of IH Rostrum Club; Box 3, File 7.8, Surveys and Statistics

Chapter Five

The 1990s

Brendon Drain

Of the many events that make up the IH year, the Candlelight Ceremony and Dinner is arguably the most important. A ritual derived from the 'mother-house' in New York, the dinner concluded with representatives of each nationality in IH symbolically 'passing the light' by way of lighting a candle and reciting, in their own language, the pledge: 'As light begets light, so love, friendship and goodwill are passed from one to another. We who come from many nations to live in fellowship in International House, promise one another to pass the light wherever we go.'

The Candlelight Ceremony of 1999 did not follow the script. Instead of merely reciting the pledge, many representatives altered the words imbuing the pledge with their culture, nationality and, most importantly of all, themselves. The representative of New Zealand, Matt Ottignon, read the pledge backwards. Nicos Pavlides, the Cypriot representative, began his pledge with a short synopsis of his country's history, starting with the fall of Troy in 1183 BC. Andrés Gómez de Silva Garza, the Senior Resident who happened to be on call that night with the recently introduced Senior Resident cordless phone, had another resident call him as he approached the dais and make out that he had locked himself out of his room just before Andrés recited the pledge as the representative of Mexico. The evening was then capped off by the Australian representative, Emma Farrell, who 'translated' the pledge into colloquial Australian and concluded with the memorable statement: 'And I'll seeya on the way to Gundagai!'

These acts could easily be interpreted as childish. They were not. They were the manifestation of the culture that pervaded IH during the 1990s: a culture of friendship and openness amongst residents that encouraged the breaking down of cultural barriers through shared experience and by having fun. It was a culture that challenged residents to resolve issues between themselves rather than resort to formal structures and to make IH and its formalities their own and not those of a previous generation. This culture brought with it a sense of independence and empowerment. IH was their home and they shaped it in their image. This made for a resident-focussed decade.

The character of the House during this period owed much to the policies and practice of the man whose presence dominated IH during the 1990s: Geoffrey Andrews. Born in Surrey, England, in 1940, Geoffrey Andrews was educated in the UK and spent time at Cambridge University during the 1950s. He emigrated to Australia in 1971 and after stints in Western Australia, New Zealand and Melbourne, finally settled in New South Wales where he was Headmaster of The Armidale School for four years. He was appointed Director of International House in 1987.

Approachable and genuinely interested in the well-being of residents, 'Mr Andrews', as he was respectfully known ('Mr A' behind his back), left an indelible impression on many residents. Recognising that IH was a diverse community he sought to encourage independence and self-reliance in the residents by adopting a policy of interfering as little as possible in their lives and challenging them to create a successful community. As he told the SUIHAA Newsletter in 1999: 'There should be help there if they need it but one shouldn't assume that they're going to need it … They know that they are expected to behave like adults.' This attitude sprang from his time at a Cambridge University college where many of his fellow residents had served in the British armed forces in Malaya, Kenya or during the Suez Crisis: it was an adult institution whose residents could look after and manage themselves. His attitude towards managing a university residential college was reinforced by the experiences of his son, Richard, who had been an IH resident and Chairman of IHMA during the mid-eighties. In Geoffrey Andrews's view, the resources for a successful community lay within the resident-body itself and there was little need for outside interference. It was an attitude which came to define IH during the 1990s.

The diversity of the resident body was perceived as vital to the interests of the House. This was its greatest strength, one which allowed people from a wide array of backgrounds to interact with others of different cultures, gender or age.

Whilst the diverse nature of IH was a constant, the nature of that diversity was anything but constant, despite the best intentions of the IH Council and administration. Out of a resident population of some two hundred, the intention was (as it had been for some time) for a rough balance in the numbers of Australian and international residents and between women and men. A feature of these years had become the difficulty in attracting Australian students. During its first three decades, as noted in earlier chapters, approximately 40 per cent of IH's residents were Australian. By 1990 that figure had dropped to 35 per cent and it continued to fall, reaching a nadir of 22 per cent in March 1996. The situation was partially rectified in the later part of the decade, but the figure still hovered below 30 per cent. Reasons for this decline were varied (and are still being thought through to this day). The prevailing economic climate of the nineties interacted to some degree with the historic Australian tendency to go directly to university from school — the idea of a 'gap year', so popular in recent years, had not yet come into vogue. Like Graeme de Graaff before him, Geoffrey Andrews's informal policy was not to admit residents straight from school (and he has commented that he only ever accepted one such application in his time as Director), so this had the effect of significantly reducing the number of Australians eligible for admission.

There were also other factors at play. There was, for instance, a misconception in many quarters that IH was primarily a hall of residence for international students, something that would influence Australians of a more insular outlook to shy away (the flip side was that most of the Australian residents made a deliberate decision to come to IH and were therefore more likely to contribute to the community). The reduction in numbers may also have been connected to the increase in non-college accommodation offered during the 1990s and to the cost of living at a residential college like IH. Whatever the causes, the phenomenon was not unique to Sydney IH: it was also the experience of the sister House at the University of New South Wales.

Whilst this was a concern to some, it made arguably for a more enriching residential experience. Fewer Australian residents meant a corresponding increase in international students, resulting in a more diverse array of cultures and nationalities. By the late nineties, IH constantly had over 40 nationalities, exposing residents to an almost unfathomable array of cultural experiences. This exposure often had a profound effect on those it touched and this is reflected in the recollections of residents. The 1997 New South Wales' Rhodes Scholar, Dhananjayan 'Danny' Sriskandarajah, recalls:

> For me, my time at IH was important in reminding me how important an internationalist perspective was. I think Sydney University (and Australia more generally perhaps) can get very insular but IH was a place that really reminded me how important it was to get out and see the world. So, in an indirect way, being at IH encouraged me to drop the law bit of my degrees and apply for scholarships to go overseas. And I was lucky enough to get the Rhodes.

Conan Elphicke, a resident in 1991, has similarly fond recollections: '1991 was a seminal year for me. I had a marvellous time, met a superb range of excellent people, many of whom I remained in contact with for years, and I was influenced for the better.'

It is also questionable whether the need for half the residents to be Australian was as relevant as it had been when IH's doors opened in 1967. Whilst no one could claim that Australia of 1990 could rival New York or London as a multicultural melting pot, it was far removed from the Australia of 1967, at which time the White Australia policy was still in evidence. Mainstream Australian culture was far less the predominantly Anglo-Saxon-Celtic one of the immediate post-war period and Sydney was fast becoming a truly international city — culminating in the Olympic Games of 2000. Of course, this also raised the problem of the very definition of an 'Australian resident'. By this time, many Australian residents had strong family links with other nations and cultures. Arguably this made the paradigm of the Australian–international split redundant.

This cultural and national diversity was enhanced by a balance of young and old, women and men. The average age hovered consistently around 26 (over the decade it was actually 26.2 years) and there was a general balance between postgraduates and undergraduates. This all ensured there was a healthy mix of leadership, maturity and youthfulness.

When the International House movement originated in the 1920s, one of the more controversial aspects was the then-radical concept of men and women living in the same residence. Whilst attitudes had changed (somewhat) by the nineties, this idea could still be controversial and in certain cultures frowned upon (particularly the idea of shared bathrooms). I well remember that one resident managed to keep from his family for the duration of his long stay in the House the fact that IH had mixed accommodation. He even managed to keep up the charade when he returned to IH with his parents to celebrate his graduation — explaining the presence of women as a 'recent thing' brought about by the new Director, Dr Ruth Shatford.

The generally equal numbers of women and men that existed throughout the decade was an integral part of the IH experience during that time and led to the formation of many intercultural romances, some of which flourish to this day. The number of relationships was both amusing and inspiring — amusing in that late in the decade, when IHMA was seeking a motto for its annual tee-shirt, one resident could seriously suggest the phrase: 'International House: International Affairs under one roof' — an interesting use of double-entendre that, to my mind, neatly encapsulates the period … in all respects. The number of these relationships was also inspiring, as there is no better agent in overcoming prejudice and intolerance. During the decade there were successful relationships between people of different nationalities that, outside IH, were openly hostile to each other. It is a shame that no accurate figures exist for the number of IH marriages celebrated during the 1990s. My guess is that there were more than several dozen. The vast majority of these marriages still exist and many have borne children.

On this note, it was during this decade that IH witnessed the first of what Americans might call 'legacy residents': the offspring of an IH union. The first of these legacy residents was Nicholas (Nick) Gotsis. The son of Demetrius Gotsis and Anne Seale, Nick, started in IH in 1998; he has been followed by others, including the current IHMA Chairperson, Daniel Ackland. The emergence of legacy residents did, of course, give rise to another conundrum: should the entry criteria for legacy residents be any different from those for other residents?

The side-effects of IH's providing accommodation for both women and men, however, could also be cruel. For many residents from overseas their time in the House was one in which 'reality' was temporarily suspended. Free from family expectations and cultural pressures, they could forge personal relationships and be a person that they could never be once their time in Sydney was up. For every successful IH marriage there were numerous relationships that ended when the residents left IH. Most of these ended amicably and are remembered fondly. However, the distressing reality is that there were some IH relationships that ended on a sad note, leaving emotional scars that no period of time could heal.

The selection of residents played an important role in the life of the House in the 1990s. It resulted in an informal and independent resident-body, characterised by irreverence and a sense of ownership of 'the House', both physical and spiritual. There was a sense of pride, IH was 'our home'. This was reflected in the often-incongruous spaces where residents met. Unlike the Houses in New York or Berkeley, where each floor contained its own meeting areas, complete with comfy chairs, television and video equipment, magazines and books, IH did not have many obvious gathering spots in readily-accessible areas. This led to residents quite literally requisitioning areas and making them their own. Following the renovations in 1996, the couches and poufs in the foyer became one such focal point, a place where residents could be sure to meet each other at virtually any time of day or night. Described by one resident of the era as a 'procrastination centre', this area was particularly popular when the night-time tea trolleys came out.

The absence of an on-site bar resulted in residents often taking over the beer gardens of two nearby pubs, 'The Duck and Swan' and 'The

Rose', both just a short walk down Cleveland Street. A night at one of these pubs — the venue for many farewells and social functions — was often a resident's first, not to mention last, memory of their time at IH. Even Geoffrey Andrews managed to end his time at IH with a round of pool on the table at 'The Rose', following his farewell 'bush-tucker' dinner in 1999, much to the delight of many residents!

As other writers have observed, the dining room also was always a key meeting point for residents. Its round tables and lack of hierarchy facilitated discussion. Unsurprisingly, the subjects discussed around the tables often concerned the state of the food being served. Food, as we know, has been a source of consternation throughout IH's short history and this decade was no exception. Despite this, the food was not so bad — if one takes into account the amount residents actually paid for each meal. The real problem was the sameness of the meals, a state well captured in this extract from an IHMA Yearbook of the period:

> Friday 6.30. Soccer is just about over and we head to the IH dining room anticipating what is for dinner. You see the food isn't that bad here where we live but as my grandfather used to say 'sometimes you get tired of the same old shit'. How right the old man was. For tonight was just one of those nights… I stared at the pork chops on my plate… I glanced towards the green cordial… I knew I would miss this many years from now when I'd look back. The cordials had become part of me. I knew all that … But tonight I just couldn't take it anymore.

At times it seemed that there was no escape from the sameness, particularly after the decision was made to change caterers from Fisher Catering to Eurest in 1998. Shortly thereafter Eurest acquired Fisher Catering.

The coffee room next door to the dining room was another important meeting place. Perhaps it had something to do with its close proximity to the fridges where the late dinners were stored; or maybe it was the magazine racks. Or was it the existence of *those* pictures which have since been replaced (the Bondi beach scene was a particular favourite of some residents)? Whatever it was, the coffee room made for a bustling scene, particularly around exam time when its popularity was unsurpassed.

One final area that is worthy of note is the roof of the main building. During the 1990s this was a far cry from the five-star 'Rooftop Leisure Centre' that exists today. It was a more spartan affair in keeping with the generally stark feeling of the main building, but nonetheless it was a

17½ residents squeeze round a dining table, 1995
(Source: Andrés Gómez de Silva Garza)

popular meeting place where residents could chill out over a VB beer and gaze out on the spectacular views of Sydney. And, in true Anzac spirit, residents would make up for the lack of outdoor furniture by lugging up an assortment of chairs and pillows (and sometimes including the foyer couches and poufs) to make the place a bit more comfortable.

This ownership of space could, however, result in problems. Again, unlike the International Houses in New York and Berkeley, IH was not neatly divided into residential and public (that is, not resident-exclusive) areas. This meant that the space used to host public events was often considered 'home' and, therefore 'private', by residents. Residents who were incredibly welcoming to each other were often less than receptive to the idea of sharing their 'home' with people they had not invited — particularly when it meant that they could not have access to facilities such as the pool or television rooms. This had significant ramifications later in the decade when Jill McRae was in charge of what was, in hindsight, the unenviable task of getting the external program off the ground — a subject to which I will come later.

The spaces where residents met became the points where ideas were discussed. Despite the numerous high-profile political and social events that occurred during the 1990s, it would be misleading to suggest that IH was a hive of intellectual discourse. By and large residents were more likely to be interested in the latest IH coupling or plot developments in *Beverley Hills 90210* or *Melrose Place* than politics. Football was also the subject of much discussion, particularly during the World Cups of 1990, 1994 and 1998, when residents gathered around televisions late at night during 'study breaks' for their imminent mid-term exams. In fact the various World Cups were only rivalled as subjects of interest during the decade by the frenzy that followed the death of Diana, Princess of Wales in August 1997. In what was one of the most extraordinary weeks in recent history, much of western society (particularly the UK) went into a state of hysteria. IH was not immune from this; many residents filled the Wool Room to watch her funeral at Westminster Abbey on the large movie screen. This can be contrasted with the lack of enthusiasm evident at the time of the referendum on the republic two years later.

Popular culture, gossip and sport thus provided the context for the majority of discussions, not politics. The significance of this should not be overlooked. Many a strong and lasting intercultural friendship was founded on such trivial initial foundations. And with friendship came understanding. A Mexican friend of mine recounted to me in vivid detail an occasion on which he watched an episode of *South Park* entitled 'Mexican Staring Frog of Southern Sri Lanka' with a large group of Sri Lankan and other residents. They were all convulsed with laughter after the main theme of the episode became apparent — and, more apparent still, the irony of the mix of people who were watching. Being able to laugh at yourself was something that the IH of the nineties was all about.

However, that is not to say that residents' conversations never rose above trivial subjects. IH was a truly international space populated by a diverse and laid-back group of people — the sort of people with whom you could discuss a topical issue as well as enjoy a good laugh. One issue that was discussed during the early nineties was the issue of the wording of IH's motto: 'That brotherhood may prevail'. This, of course, was one of John Rockefeller Junior's ideas and connected IH to its 'mother-house' in New York. However, the world of the 1920s was far removed from that of the early nineties when the women's movements of the previous three decades had condemned the use of language that helped to perpetuate inequalities. Feeling on this issue was very strong and at the Flag Ceremony and Dinner of 1991 many residents refused to recite the motto whilst holding their country's flag and instead substituted what they considered to be a neutral alternative for 'brotherhood'. In the yearbook of that year, two residents wrote a paper in favour of change, arguing that there was a need to have a motto 'which residents [could] relate to as embodying the principles of International House'. The contributors were unaware that they had already won. Consideration was given as early as 1990 to the changing norms and attitudes of residents. By 1993 these changes were in effect, with 'fellowship' replacing 'brotherhood'.

There were other subjects that evoked at times intense discussion. IH was not, after all, cocooned from the real world. The display of flags at official IH functions was a particularly sensitive matter as many residents wanted the display of their nation's flag as they knew it, as opposed to being constrained by what was officially recognised by the Australian government. (During the decade this was an issue in respect of the Palestinian and Taiwanese flags particularly.) Nevertheless, despite the existence of many potentially explosive issues, the decade was marked by a lack of real conflict amongst residents. This was quite remarkable given the potentially divisive events that occurred during the decade, including the horrific atrocities in Rwanda and the former Yugoslavia, and the impeachment of the US President Bill Clinton in 1998. There were probably several reasons for this and the fact that many residents were more interested in trifling matters undoubtedly came into play. It did, however, have a lot to do with the culture Geoffrey Andrews had instilled, which encouraged the resolution of tensions between residents. Residents debated subjects, often robustly; however, at the end of the day, some type of consensus was usually reached, often following mediation by third parties including Senior Residents and members of the residents' association.

Another facet of resident life was the tendency to make the functions in the IH calendar their own. The 'success' of a year was invariably connected to the ability of a year's residents to manage those functions, something that was, in turn, directly connected to the quality of resident leaders. They invariably came from two groups: the Senior Residents and the IHMA. Life for a Senior Resident cannot have been easy. Apart from often being woken after hours by residents who had locked themselves out of their rooms, as de facto staff members Senior Residents could find themselves in an unenviable position in disputes between residents and the IH administration. They also had to turn a selective blind eye to some of the antics of residents, something reflected in a number of yearbook entries: no, they did not miss the heater extension cords that mysteriously snaked out of rooms to external power points.

The position of the Senior Residents also meant that the leadership role performed by them was an informal and often unrecognised one. They frequently worked behind the scenes to resolve conflicts and encourage participation in IH life and in this connection IH was lucky to have some remarkable Senior Residents during the decade. Philayrath 'PH'

Phongsavan, Kenneth Kong, Peter Revelant and Eugene Varughese, to name but a few, all contributed much to the life of the House in the 1990s and are fondly remembered by their fellow residents. Residents of 1998 recall that Senior Resident Sangeeta Shah and Fang Yee Chee (the 1997 IHMA Chairperson), a doctor and medical student respectively, took the initiative after a resident had collapsed with a cerebral haemorrhage and drove the resident to hospital when the ambulance was late to arrive (the resident in question is alive and well). Numerous similar examples could be recounted to highlight the ability of the Senior Residents to rally the resident-body to deal with serious problems without outside help whenever they arose.

On a more social level, Peter Revelant and Eugene Varughese spent many an hour battling that most IH of eccentricities, 'IH time' (the state where IH ran half-an-hour behind the rest of Sydney) to organise the informal football games played on Victoria Park across City Road. Another important aspect of residential life, these informal 'kick arounds' proved to be a key catalyst in bringing the different cultures at IH together. Football really was 'the world game'.

Encouraged by Geoffrey Andrews, the Senior Residents played a crucial role in organising many excursions out of Sydney in the IH mini-bus (which was named 'Basil' by residents in 1997). Many people enjoyed their first taste of Australian life outside of Sydney on such trips. Itineraries often included stopovers at the family homes of Australian residents and staff. The Senior Residents were ably assisted in organising such adventures by the various 'mafias' that sprang up in the House. No, the mafias were not members of secret societies who met undercover down in the dark room to plot the downfall of the IHMA. 'Mafia' was the endearing term used by residents to describe a particularly large national contingent. So, for example, there was not only the Austrian mafia of 1996 and 1997, but also the so-called Sri Lankan mafia that held sway during the mid-nineties. The Aussie adventures of the mafias were the stuff of legend. In 1993 an 'anonymous Sri Lankan contingent' decided to hire a bus and rove around Australia. When the time came to wash the mini-bus at an automated car wash, chaos ensued:

> Slowly, they drove into the car wash and heard the detergent brushes lowering onto the roof. The brushes sloshed away the dirt and grim [sic] and kept lowering. Firmly, the brushes started to clean the paint job off the roof. Even more firmly the brushes started to push the roof in. Panicked, there was nothing for the Sri Lankans to do except wait till the wash cycle had finished. Finally the wax

had dried to a gleaming sheen and the bus was started up.
After a hideous eardrum rupturing sound, the bus ground
to a halt. Stuck fast, the quick witted Sri Lankans decided
the only way to get out was to let the tyres down.

The other, more official, source of residential leadership was the residents' association, the IHMA, which has figured in earlier chapters. This was a challenging decade, with the association at times struggling for leadership and support. This was not the result of resident apathy: it was more a case of changing economic times as residents were having to pay for their university education and were no longer guaranteed a job after graduating. Extra-curricular activities thus often took a back seat.

The organisation also had to deal with various crises. A particularly noteworthy one was a financial crisis in 1997, which placed funding from the University's Student Union under threat (one consequence of which was that no IHMA yearbook was published in 1997). This crisis was only averted by the strong leadership of the 1998 IHMA Committee, particularly the Treasurer, Kate Pritchett, who spent many hours reconstructing the IHMA's books and negotiating with Student Union officials — another example of the resident-body overcoming problems by drawing on the skills and talents of their own.

Kinna Choy from Hong Kong, Food Fair, 1998
(Source: Andrés Gómez de Silva Garza)

IHMA hosted many events during the decade, including trips to Bronte beach for barbeques, Harbour cruises, numerous discos, floor parties, paintball skirmishes and other sporting events. The International Food Fair was one of the highlights of living in IH. Despite the logistical problems involved in getting it organised, the wide variety of dishes available meant that even the pickiest eaters found something to their liking, and a chance to eat food that was not prepared by the regular IH caterer was always considered a bonus. Each participating country or region was given a portion of the Food Fair budget (usually way too small), though exactly how much this amounted to was often not known until after the event. This was because often countries decided to merge to form collaborations, such as 'the Indian subcontinent' — India, Pakistan, Bangladesh, Sri Lanka, and the Maldives — or 'Greater China' — Hong Kong, Taiwan and the People's Republic of China — to prepare something together; or collaborators would decide to separate, sometimes only hours before the Food Fair was to open. Most participating countries found creative ways to take full advantage of their limited budget, or would add some of their own money to the IHMA funds out of national pride and the desire to produce top-quality dishes.

Kitchens in the Maze units and even the small kitchens with limited space and equipment in the Main Building and East and Elkin Wings were staked out by cooking contingents several hours in advance of the Food Fair in order to ensure access to the necessary cooking facilities. Sometimes IHMA would try to organise this aspect of the Food Fair, but sometimes it was 'every man/woman/country for him/her/itself' and 'first come first served'. The attention given to posters, national dress, and other decorative aspects of the Food Fair sometimes rivalled the preparation of the food itself. The Australians of IH would often serve Vegemite sandwiches, musk sticks, and whatever meat they could find to put on the 'barbie'. The Irish contingent would often provide Guinness — certainly available in Australia, but not an everyday IH drink ('VB' and Tooheys New were probably the most popular IH beverages). The Danish group once served dried whale blubber from the Faroe Islands — not a common delicacy in Australia, and probably illegal. And these are just a few examples. In other words, the food and everything surrounding the event was as varied as the residents, who found the Food Fair to be the perfect occasion to show their resourcefulness and give free rein to their creative spirits — just the right ingredients for success!

Another memorable event was the International Night — which by the mid-nineties was a completely separate event from the Food Fair

The Malaysian dance, International Night, 1998
(Source: Andrés Gómez de Silva Garza)

(they had often previously been held simultaneously). International Night could not be described as a professional affair. Instead, it was another example of residents proudly being themselves and representing their nation — or other nations, as residents were often drafted into the performances of other nationalities, such as the perennially popular Greek dances — in any way they saw fit. It was very much the residents' production, with all the acts scripted and produced by them, with little external input. The diversity of the acts at such events was often breathtaking. In 1994, for example, the MCs, Norman Ferrandiz and Colleen McInerney, introduced an array of acts which included a Lebanese belly dance, a Punjabi folk song, a north-eastern Thai folk dance, Scottish Highland dancing, a moon kite dance from the Malaysian residents, a Philippino folk dance, a Sri Lankan cultural dance and a karate demonstration by Gaku Yamagata, Yoshio Maki and Ryusuke Kimura from Japan.

On the social side of things, another big event in the IH year was the Inter-floor Games. The subject of often intense rivalry between residents, the games consisted of such distinguished events as tug-of-war, Victoria Park foot races, beer sculling (no, not what it sounds like — see the photograph, next page), the tower run, ice-cream-eating competitions, arm wrestling and the often hilarious treasure hunt — which invariably ended up with residents cross-dressing or in togas (or, in 1995, both).

117

Beer-sculling, IH style — through a straw! 1998
(Source: Andrés Gómez de Silva Garza)

The games gave rise to many a legend. Chief amongst them is Sanjaya 'Sanjay' Ekanayake, whose waste-disposal-like approach to the ice-cream-eating competition made him invincible during the later part of the decade. Whilst most competitors actually ate the ice-cream, Sanjay adopted the strategy of tilting his head back and instructing his 'feeder' to shovel the ice-cream into his mouth. Swallowing had no part in this strategy, which resulted in an unbeaten run from 1996 through to 1998. The legend was only finally defeated in 1999 thanks to the devious cunning of Sanjay's friend, Eric Gatabaki, who, after cottoning on to the fact that there was a limit to the amount of ice cream that could fit into the human mouth, increased the amount that needed to be consumed. This led to comical scenes when Sanjay, realising that his winning streak was in jeopardy, at one point grabbed the plate of remaining ice-cream out of the hands of his 'feeder' and shoved it (not to mention the plastic spoon) into his mouth. Alas, this desperate act did not succeed and Sanjay's winning run was broken.

Another institution of the social calendar was the annual IH Ball. Despite suffering from a lack of numbers at times during the decade, there was a spectacular revival in 1998 when a sell-out was organised at the Centrepoint Tower. The ball has gone from strength to strength ever since.

An important 'ice-breaker' for residents was the annual 'Assassination Game'. The premise of the game is simple: participants begin with a 'weapon' (actually a piece of paper) with the name of their target 'victim'. They must 'assassinate' victims without any witnesses by touching them and uttering a phrase, which tended to be drawn from popular culture — usually from a movie or television show. In 1994 Arnold Schwarzenegger fans revelled in uttering the words 'Hasta la vista, baby' when 'terminating' their prey. The following year residents struck down their victims 'With great anger and furious vengeance', a homage to Quentin Tarantino. And, perhaps in keeping with the more cynical attitudes of the late nineties, in 1998 residents competing in the *X Files*-themed game dispatched their opponents with the foreboding 'Everything dies'. (Sadly there was no *Titanic*-themed assassination game, residents preferring to satisfy their Kate Winslet and Leonardo di Caprio-inspired urges by 'doing the Titanic' on Harbour cruises. But that's another story.) When a 'kill' was made the assassin took the victim's 'weapon', thus acquiring the victim's target. The 'kills' were arranged in a circle such that as participants were killed, the circle of remaining assassins became smaller and smaller until only one person remained: the winner. However, possibly even more prestigious than winning was being the participant with the most kills, the so-called 'serial killer' (or when the serial killer was of a more hyperactive bent, the 'psycho killer'). The record holder for the most kills was Richard Sematimba, with thirteen kills in the *James Bond*-themed game of 1996.

As one can imagine, the format ensured that some residents began the second semester (the Assassination Game being often held at the start of that semester) in an almost-paranoid state, with many people adopting extreme measures to avoid being 'assassinated'. This state led to many memorable escapes during the 1990s when people sought to evade their prospective assassins. These included the comical: such as the resident who, after being surprised whilst exiting the shower, dropped his towel and ran naked down the corridor to his room (one could not be assassinated while naked); and the disturbing: such as the resident who pulled out a knife on his would-be assassin in the main tower's staircase.

In addition to organising social events for the residents, IHMA also played a crucial role in facilitating the relationship between IH residents and those of the other colleges at Sydney University. Unfortunately, throughout much of the nineties (particularly the later years), this relationship could be one of mutual distrust. From the IH perspective, this may to some extent be traced to the evening of 23 August 1991, the date of the infamous toga party.

It is somewhat ironic that the events of that night had been preceded by a push for some time by many IH residents for closer relations with the other Sydney University colleges. Despite opposition and dire warnings from some sections of the House, consent was given for IHMA to host an inter-college party and excited residents publicised the event (and 'cheap beer') by scrawling chalk notices around the campus. This led to a strong turnout by some of the less desirable sections of the college crowd, who promptly went on something of a rampage: barging into residents' rooms, damaging toilets, setting off fire hydrants and creating havoc. If the event itself did not harm the relationship irreparably, the aftermath certainly did. The bill for the damage came to $1989, which was not covered by IH's insurance policy as it fell under the category 'due to wilful or reckless acts'. Despite IHMA's allegedly obtaining a commitment from the residents' association of the college most closely concerned in the mayhem that they would cover these costs, in 1992 IHMA paid $1000 of the outstanding account with IH to cover the balance.

The unease was exacerbated by the publicity that some of the more extreme examples of college behaviour received during the decade. During 1991, for example, *Honi Soit,* the SRC's weekly publication, reproduced extracts from the St John's College orientation magazine, *Yakai,* which were so offensive that they caused uproar. This was followed later in the decade by the book, *Finishing School for Blokes* by Peter Cameron, the former Principal of St Andrew's College, which contained many damaging revelations of college 'hazing' rituals.

The wary relationship was also evident on other levels. As already remarked, IH found it increasingly difficult to attract Australian residents during the decade. This was not helped by several colleges in the mid-nineties advertising that IH was a hall for international students in the first instance. College residents started to look upon IH residents as something of a strange breed and I can still recall many college friends of mine exclaiming 'Where?!' or 'Why?!' after I had told them where I was living.

Given the distrust and misunderstanding, it is not surprising that the Sydney University colleges became the great 'other' in the IH consciousness. They became the vacuum into which all the negative aspects associated with twenty-something communal living were poured, creating an antithesis of what IH residents considered themselves to be. In light of the ingrained nature of this typecasting it was (and still is) extremely difficult, if not impossible, to avoid it; I readily admit to falling into the trap here.

As with most generalisations this representation was simplistic and contributed to the distrust that existed. There were differences between IH and the other colleges. The average age of IH residents was higher and the spread of ages was greater. For every eighteen-year-old for whom living at IH was one of the first experiences of living away from home (or school), there was someone in their later twenties with considerable life experience. Older residents almost naturally kept an eye out for the younger residents and in doing so helped to prevent the more extreme examples of college (mis)behaviour from occurring. IH thus avoided the initiation traditions, such as introducing your pet brick, or the 'fresher walk', which were hallmarks of the colleges (although admittedly IH did have some other rituals of its own, such as the 'sock race', introduced by Swedish residents, which formed the basis of many a farewell later in the decade). IH also had a far wider array of cultures than the other Sydney University colleges. IH was a truly international space on a campus that at times was quite insular. This could not help but have an impact of the behaviour of residents.

But as these observations suggest, there were similarities. We should not delude ourselves into thinking that the alcohol-fuelled behaviour associated with 'college life' did not exist at IH. It did — although not on the same scale as at some of the other residential colleges. Moreover, contrary to popular IH belief, there actually were some intelligent, enlightened and well-travelled college residents, who transcended the beer-swilling yobbo depicted in caricatures. Indeed, if one looked closely, there were as many similarities between IH and the other Sydney University colleges as there were differences, making the schism that existed, at least at a residential level, all the more tragic. IH residents would have certainly benefited from having access to the inter-college tutor system. Further, too, many residents would have enjoyed representing IH in the inter-col sporting competitions, particularly football. Whilst IH took part in some events in this competition at the beginning of the decade with a certain amount of success — in 1991 IH defeated St John's College 4–3 in the inter-col football competition — this participation did not last. IH's non-participation was usually put down to resistance by many of the colleges to IH's selective participation (IH could never field teams in all events) on the basis that it tended to skew the results. Whilst there was an element of truth to this, there were perhaps deeper reasons linked to failure to converse and relate to residents of the other colleges at a social level (which was possibly the natural consequence of the drop in the number of Australian residents at IH). It is an irresistible speculation: is this an example of IH, collectively, displaying the type of prejudice towards others that it so actively sought to eradicate?

The relationship with the colleges was not completely severed, however. Geoffrey Andrews attended meetings with other administrative heads of colleges throughout these years. In addition, IH residents continued to compete, with some success, at the annual inter-col oration, with IH representatives winning in 1991 (Conan Ephicke) and 1995 (Ben Waters).

The interaction between IH and the other International Houses, particularly those in Australia, was another disappointment. Whilst the decade began promisingly in this regard, with IHMA reporting to Council in 1992 of approaches to establish an Australia-wide network of IHMAs, the grand tradition of the corroboree — where residents of the Australian International Houses would meet for a week of fun and activities — went into an almost terminal decline during the decade. This was particularly tragic as by 1990 there were eight International Houses spread across Australia.

If the nineties posed numerous challenges for the resident leaders of IH, the same can be said for the IH Council. Consisting solely of volunteers who gave up their valuable spare time, the Council comprised people of considerable energy and experience. Among those who had the difficult task of guiding IH through what was at times a frustrating period, and (perhaps to some) a disappointing one, was Brian Farmer. An IH alumnus and successful businessman, Brian Farmer was the first alumnus to be appointed to the IH Council and served as Chair from 1994 to 1996. Alongside that other great IH philanthropist and leader, Ian Hudson, he had also been one of the key drivers behind building the Log Cabin in the Belanglo State Forest during the 1970s. He was, therefore, naturally concerned when a decline in residents' use of the cabin during the early nineties became apparent. This decline, which may have been linked to the 'backpacker murders' of the era, was so significant that by the mid-nineties there were suggestions that the log cabin may have served its purpose as far as residents were concerned. Brian Farmer, ably assisted by a number of dedicated alumni, worked steadily over the next few years to upgrade and maintain the Log Cabin. The facility that exists today — one which has been enjoyed by successive generations of IH residents and alumni — stands as a testament to their work.

Another key figure from the decade was Richard Wilson. With a background as a senior member of the Australian Foreign Affairs

Department, Richard Wilson endeared himsclf to residents by lodging at IH whilst in Sydney for Council meetings. This made him something of a rarity at IH, an 'oldie' who was actually considered 'one of us'. This was never better demonstrated than in the dining room at meal times. Whereas residents would often avoid older non-residents who turned up to dinner, Richard Wilson always found himself at a table full of residents. If there was any truth in the statement that Council members were out of touch (a criticism that was levelled at the Council at various times during the decade), it certainly did not apply to Richard Wilson.

As a member initially appointed by the University Senate to act as its representative, Daphne Kok was another prominent member of Council during the decade. The increasingly interventionist role of the University in the day-to-day affairs of IH was one of the key trends of the nineties, with the University's interest increasing as its funding became more dependent on full-fee-paying overseas students. Daphne Kok's role was therefore a critical one.

One of the problems faced by the IH Council during this decade was the role of SUIHAA and what had, by now, become the sizable Sydney-based alumni community. These were difficult years for alumni organisations in general, with their relevance being questioned and reinterpreted. SUIHAA did not escape this scrutiny. By the mid-nineties it was becoming increasingly clear that the role and structure of SUIHAA needed to be reassessed and publicised. When leaving IH, many residents were not bothering to register with SUIHAA — something due in part to a concern that they would be subjected to requests for donations. The rapid development during this time of the Internet and email also meant that many ex-residents had little need to rely on SUIHAA to keep in touch with other alumni. Indeed, the number of 'IH reunions', involving sometimes upwards of 50 former residents, suggests that, in keeping with the informal and resident-focussed nature of the decade, SUIHAA's relevance as a networking agent for departing residents was arguably less important to IH residents of the nineties than to earlier generations of residents.

The IH Council and some key figures at SUIHAA during the decade did take steps to address these concerns. In 1994, the then SUIHAA President, 'PH' Phongsavan, presented to Council a wide-ranging report into the future role of SUIHAA; this included many recommendations, such as formalising the publication of two alumni magazines per year, and IH's providing SUIHAA with funding and an office. Many of the recommendations were acted upon by the Council, with funding to the association coming from the imposition of an automatic SUIHAA levy on departing residents and an office being provided in 1999. Perhaps more controversially, IH provided SUIHAA with administrative funding for the publication of its magazine — something that rankled with some residents who felt they were subsidising a publication that had little to do with them. SUIHAA also responded to changing technologies and in 1998 set up an Internet site which allowed alumni to contact each other.

Another challenge facing the Council was the state of the IH buildings. When the House was first opened in 1967 the buildings had, believe it or not, been considered 'state of the art'. However, by 1990, those same buildings were nearly twenty-five years old and showing their age. Resident surveys commissioned in the late eighties and early nineties highlighted the general dinginess of rooms, with the state of the carpet coming in for particular attention. And then there was the lift. The IH lift was one of a kind. Whereas most lifts stop on proper levels, the IH lift had a mind of its own and frequently decided to stop mid-floor, stay there for several hours before almost free-falling several floors down to the basement, much to amusement of onlookers and the terror of the poor unsuspecting residents trapped inside. This decidedly IH in-joke became even funnier in 1993 with the premiere of Steven Spielberg's Oscar-winning motion picture, *Schindler's List* — the name of the company that maintained the lift was, believe it or not, Schindlers Lifts.

The shortcomings of the Wool Room and Rotunda were also under scrutiny. Of particular concern was the lack of a fire escape, which contravened New South Wales statutory requirements. The Wool Room also lacked separate facilities and could not be separated from the residential sections of IH. This limited the possibilities of staging external events, taking away a potentially valuable source of income.

With IH's silver anniversary fast approaching, the Council determined that something needed to be done to ensure that these faults were rectified. A Council sub-committee was established, architects were consulted and an ambitious refurbishment was planned as part of a 'Silver Anniversary Project'. The proposed re-development plans included a 'face lift' of the study bedrooms, an expansion of the entrance and foyer and a refurbishment of the Wool Room and coffee lounge. Of these, the plans for the Wool Room were the most dramatic, the proposals including the creation of a second entrance via the Seymour Centre and a passageway between the main residential block and the Rotunda which, along with the proposed changes to the entrance, meant that the Wool Room could become self-contained and separate from the residential areas, so alleviating residents' concerns about security when the Wool Room hosted events that were not resident-specific.

Such an ambitious project came with a significant price tag — in excess of three million dollars — and Kenneth Clemens and Stuart Cameron, Financial Consultants, were appointed at a nominal fee to assist the fund-raising campaign. The decision was made to focus IH's fund-raising efforts on South-east Asia. This focus made sense. The idea of Australia as part of Asia was an important political theme of the late eighties and early nineties and, under the Bob Hawke and Paul Keating Labor governments, Australia was repositioning itself away from its historic partners in Europe and the USA towards Asia. The economies of many South-east Asian countries were booming at the time, along with Japan; the so-called tigers (Singapore, Hong Kong, Taiwan and South Korea), Thailand and Malaysia were emerging as financial superpowers in their own right. The fact that IH historically drew a large percentage of its residents from these countries meant that there was much confidence that the fund-raising campaign would be successful. Numerous companies were contacted and in September 1991 Geoffrey Andrews and Kenneth Clemens undertook a fund-raising trip to Singapore, Kuala Lumpur, Hong Kong and Bangkok, where they made personal representations to eight corporate boards.

In retrospect, Council concluded that there had been two reasons for the lukewarm response. The first was that it might have been easier to get support from some sources if the appeal had been for a brand-new building, rather than for modifications and extensions to an existing one. The second reason was that some potential donations were contingent on IH's reserving a specified number of places for students from the donor's country. This condition could, clearly, not be met.

By February 1992, the IH Council had resigned itself to the failure to raise significant donations from Asia. Council was also of the view that a full-scale fund-raising campaign in Australia would consume significant resources that in light of the difficult economic conditions in Australia at the time could not be justified. The project was re-assessed as a medium-term goal and the more ambitious elements of the Silver Anniversary Project were shelved. It was decided that parts of the project should be implemented in a piecemeal fashion, with the urgently needed improvements to the Wool Room (those necessary to comply with fire regulations) given priority. In 1993 it was decided to provide fire escapes from the Wool Room and upper levels of the Rotunda and to upgrade the toilet facilities. In that same year private telephones were installed in each room. Other changes were made during 1995 and 1996 to the foyer, with the IHMA shop being moved to its current location near the lift, security doors installed separating the residential area from the entrance and the entrance foyer enlarged to include those comfy couches that soon became a central meeting point (or procrastination area, depending on your viewpoint) for residents.

The Silver Anniversary celebrations thus went ahead in 1992 without the announcement of a major renovation project. The anniversary dinner was held on 27 July 1992, with the Governor of New South Wales, His Excellency Rear Admiral Peter Sinclair, attending. It provided those present with an opportunity to reflect on what International House had achieved and on the individuals who had made it what it had become. In his speech Geoffrey Andrews made particular mention of Rosalie McCutcheon, who had recently passed away, and Rosemary Berrick, the long-serving honorary IH archivist. A series of anniversary lectures were also held, including one given by His Honour Justice Michael Kirby, then President of the New South Wales Court of Appeal and later a Justice of the Australian High Court.

The failure of the Silver Anniversary Project and the lack of a clearer divide between the Rotunda and the residential block had an impact on the decade's other ambitious project: the external program. The external program was in many ways the decade's 'noble experiment'. However, despite all the time and attention devoted to it, the outcome was to be a disappointing one — for very much the same reasons as the lack of success of the International Centre in the 1970s.

The program represented an imaginative response to the situation of IH in the early nineties. With the general concerns about the apathy shown by some residents towards IH programs such as the Food Fair and International Night, it was suggested that the resident community needed assistance to ensure that these worthwhile programs were successful. There was also a desire, reminiscent of that which was behind the idea of the International Centre in the 1970s, for IH to be more than just a residence for students from overseas. There was a wish to create a presence in the community and to be proactive in the wider University of Sydney international student community that was encouraged by the University's push to attract more full-fee-paying international students.

In 1995, Jean Cooney was engaged on a part-time basis as 'Program Facilitator'. She stayed in the role for less than a year before leaving in May 1996. The position was repackaged as that of 'External Director' and Dr Jill McRae was appointed in late 1996.

Under Jill McRae, IH was able to engage the wider community by hosting several high-profile events. The most memorable of these, and the one that attracted the most publicity, was a speech given in 1997 by José Ramos-Horta, the Nobel laureate from East Timor. During the same year a well-attended Landmine Colloquium was held at IH; this also gained publicity, partially because it attracted the attention of protesters demonstrating against the Myanmar government, which was represented at the Colloquium. But, as in the 1970s, the external program faced the difficult problem of balancing the needs of the residents with the proposed 'outreach' role of the House and in the end the two proved irreconcilable. The events were intended to attract non-residents, but because of the failure of the campaign to finance the work necessary to properly separate the Wool Room from the residential area, these events invariably resulted in a loss of amenities for residents and a certain invasion of their privacy.

One of the features of the nineties, then, was that residents were, in general, less than receptive to the idea of sharing their 'home' with people they had not invited. There was also a hint of what might be termed a generational issue here. Whereas the International Centre tended to attract international student guests, the external program attracted interest from the ever-expanding alumni community based in Sydney. These people often seemed to residents to have little in common with them, despite their best intentions.

These concerns were compounded by security threats during the mid-nineties. In 1996 there were break-ins, with nearly every room on the fifth floor being targeted one afternoon. During the mid-year vacation in 1997 the House received a bomb threat. Whilst there was no evidence that this threat was related to the colloquium on landmines being held at that time, many residents questioned the desirability of holding functions in IH that had the potential to compromise their safety.

The age of the residents was also an issue. In the chapter that follows this one, Joan Rowlands notes that with a resident median age of 25 years, it had become apparent that a full-time Program Director was no longer necessary. This was equally as true for the nineties (median age over 26), raising the issue as to whether residents needed help in organising events.

In many respects, the failure of the external program reflected the key trend of these years; a strong and independent group of residents revelled in creating a living environment of their own. It was a resident-focussed decade, not an externally-oriented one, one in which a laid-back and diverse community created a truly international space. Whilst there were a few disappointments, the overwhelming feeling of the nineties, from the residents' perspective, was one of success. By sharing in the responsibility for making their IH their own and by having fun, residents were able to show that fellowship could prevail.

Sources

I am particularly indebted to Jackie Hartley who recently reorganised the IH archives and whose summaries enabled me to overcome the tyranny of distance and complete this chapter (I am based in London). Without her assistance this would not have been possible.

I also acknowledge the support of Joan Rowlands in providing access to the back catalogue of SUIHAA Newsletters and IHMA in enabling access to the yearbooks in its collection (1990–91, 1993 and 1995–96). Sonia Montiero and Lalit Bhadresha provided copies of the 1998 and 1999 IHMA yearbooks respectively. (I understand that there were no IHMA yearbooks published in 1994 and 1997; unfortunately no copy of the 1992 yearbook was available.) I also benefited greatly from the help of Brian Farmer.

This chapter draws on the personal reflections of a number of former residents and members of the IH community, including Geoffrey Andrews, who was interviewed by John Gascoigne in October 2006, and Brian Farmer. I also benefited greatly from the comments of Andrés Gómez de Silva Garza, who reviewed early drafts of this chapter. Of course, all mistakes are mine.

IH Archives:

I made particular use of the IH Council Meeting papers 1990–99, Geoffrey Andrews's speeches 1990–99, the Silver Anniversary Project files and the files of the External Program Assistant Director/Facilitator.

Chapter Six
2000 to 2006
Joan Rowlands

In May 1999 I drove down Pennant Hills Road towards Parramatta, the butt of every impatient truck as I dawdled at each intersection to look for the turn off to Masons Drive and Tara Anglican School for Girls.

I had been given the somewhat daunting assignment of interviewing Dr Ruth Shatford, the Principal of Tara School and now Director-elect of International House of the University of Sydney, for the International House Alumni Association's Newsletter and early memories of the head of my own boarding school did not take long to surface. But my fears were soon allayed by reality: the warmth of my welcome by Ruth Shatford who, brisk, smiling and friendly, bore no resemblance to the terrorist of my youth.

Ruth Shatford was born, bred and schooled in Sydney. She read French, English and Psychology for her Arts degree at Sydney University and completed her Diploma of Education. Teaching was to be her mainstream career, but while teaching she decided that psychology would be a useful adjunct to her skills and, not content with a Master's degree in the subject, she became interested in its application to education. Realising that she needed to improve her French, she put the two together and went to Strasbourg, in France, to do her doctorate in Social Psychology applied to education.

In 1968, as a foreign student, she lived in rented accommodation with a colleague from Sydney. At postgraduate level there was little opportunity to relate to other students or to make contact with locals, so they especially valued the invitations extended to them by a French family, under one of the 'Invite a Foreign Student into Your Home' schemes. Not only did they visit this family's home in Strasbourg, they also spent time with them at their mountain retreat. In considering her appointment to International House, she saw the House as a valuable opportunity for students to meet a wide range of other nationalities, as well as Australians, in the community that develops in the House — an opportunity even more important in a large city than one the size of Strasbourg.

On her return from France, Ruth Shatford again taught in a secondary school in the state system and this was followed by three years as Deputy Headmistress at Methodist Ladies' College, Burwood. A later five years in Teacher Education at Milperra College of Advanced

Education gave her considerable experience of tertiary education before she was appointed Principal at Tara Anglican School. Now, after twenty years there, she had been considering what should be the next stage for her, somewhere she could use her experience and training yet would provide a new and sufficient challenge. She admitted to 'a capacity for boredom' and felt that so many things at Tara had recently come to a conclusion that it seemed to be an appropriate time to accept a request that she consider the position of Director at International House. The Tara School community responded very positively to her news, although somewhat taken aback and, according to her, most people's reaction was summed up bluntly in the words of the laundry lady who said, 'Gee …your letter this morning was a bit of a shock. I thought you'd be here until you died!' 'And', said Ruth, 'it was very kindly meant!'

As I left I was sure she would have looked around the quiet green oasis of landscaped grounds that she was soon to exchange for the clangour of City Road, and I wondered how keenly she would miss Tara School — but I was prepared to bet that she would not be bored.

In mid-May 1999 Ruth Shatford, who had been described in an interview for the *Sydney Morning Herald* as 'The Principal with Principles', took up her appointment as Director of Sydney University's International House. She arrived to find a host of silly rumours circulating:

L to r: Joan Rowlands (Farrar), SUIHAA President, Ruth Shatford, former Director, Rowena Danziger, Ken Coles, Council Chair, Dennis Cowdroy, Councillor and former Chair, 2003

that, coming from a girls' school, she would separate floors by gender, only admit Anglicans — and other similar, nonsensical suppositions. It did not take her long to put these fears to rest and she remembers a House that she characterises as 'having a good spirit'.

In the world outside International House, John Hamre, US Deputy Secretary of Defense, had described what he called a 'clicking time bomb for all major computer applications'. Almost forgotten now, what became known as the 'Y2K bug' became a major source of anxiety throughout the world in the approach to the new millennium — and the residents of International House were no exception. The possibility menaced the finance industry, threatened all major industries, from utilities to airlines, and billions were spent looking through application source codes to block any Y2K bug and in making computers compliant for the new millennium. On New Year's Eve 1999 main computers were switched off and back-up computers put to work; the controller of the atomic clock in Sydney sat up all night and many people elected not to fly.

In the end, as the clock ticked on into 1 January 2000 without a whimper or skipping a nanosecond, the only explosions came from showers of fireworks over Sydney Harbour Bridge, watched by excited residents on the roof of International House. The aeroplanes still flew and what had been described as an 'Electronic El Nino', which was due to usher in the new millennium and end life on earth, turned out to have been a pandemic of paranoia.

At that time there was no Assistant Director, resident or otherwise, and the Business Manager, Todd Yourell, who lived in one of the Maze units with his family, filled the role. 'He was very good', said Ruth when interviewed later, 'but I felt that it might result in a conflict or confusion of roles. A student who had been involved with Todd because of becoming behind in payments could feel awkward going to him after hours with a complaint about another resident'.

In fact she found that he did well, but although there were no specific difficulties she did not feel it to be the best of all possible situations. She also found it 'quite frightening' to realise how thinly staffed IH was, especially in the office. So in February 2000, when Todd Yourell resigned (to take up a new appointment at Brisbane International House), after deliberations with Council, not only was a new Business Manager appointed but also a part-time Assistant Business Manager. Carla Bekker was appointed Personal Assistant to the Director, Lyndley Havyatt became the receptionist and Jessica Carroll, with a history of ten years' employment at Sydney University, became the resident Assistant Director.

With this entire turnover of staff and what Ruth referred to as 'too little flesh on the bones', much corporate memory was lost and even more of the 'handing on' of traditions. However, she was to find that Jessica 'did superbly' in her new position. Although she worked at Sydney University all day, she tried to make sure that there was a daily 'overlap' with the Director. She not only attended all the Senior Residents' meetings, she also organised the return of basketball to the sports calendar. As one of the youngest Assistant Directors in the history of the House, and in the spirit of the Sydney Olympics, she took considerable pleasure in joining in the game herself.

Ruth was also to find that the three experienced Senior Residents were to become a great source of support, as was the Executive of IHMA and its Chair — who, appropriately enough in the year of the XXVII Olympiad in Sydney, was Greek: Ekaterini Lymberopoulou, more usually known as 'Kat the Chair Goddess', who, even then, was referring frequently, and with much excitement, to the next Olympics, which were to be held in Athens in 2004.

One particular student, Rex Bernado from the Philippines, who described himself as a 'differently-abled international student', felt particularly lucky to be able to study in what he called 'the right place at the right time' — Sydney in the year of the Sydney Games. As he was to write later:

> The Olympic motto — *'Citius, Altius, Fortius'* — describes in perfect simplicity the driving force which unravels in every Olympic Games …We revel in spectacular success and mourn failures. We celebrate the triumph of the human spirit against all adversities. Who can forget Eric 'the Eel' Moussambani from Equatorial Guinea, who only learnt to swim nine months earlier and took the longest time on record to complete the 100 metre freestyle…yet his mind and unflinching courage carried him to the finish line?

Rex had chosen the University of Sydney primarily because of his own physical limitations. Dependent on a wheelchair, he found that Sydney University was not only the closest to the CBD, but it also had a Disability Office and a philosophy which recognised that students with disabilities were often disadvantaged in terms of access to educational opportunities. Its policy committed the University 'to take measures to minimise the effects of disability'.

At first Rex was temporarily billeted at International House, which apparently was the only residential hall accessible for a wheelchair-user at that time. As he reported in the IHMA Yearbook, 'Upon seeing me in the Dining Hall, Dr Ruth Shatford, the Director of IH, called me into her office and warmly invited me to stay for the duration of my course'. In order to travel around the campus, he desperately needed a motorised wheelchair and was disappointed to find that the Disability Officer of the University was unable to help. Ruth Shatford, however, was and she arranged for him to be lent a motorised one, 'for free!' On completing his study he was able to say that, given 'a proper educational system and a conducive environment for learning, differently-abled students can also strive to be at par and compete with the best'.

During this year Andrés Gómez de Silva Garza, after six years in the House, wrote some interesting comments on 'some features of the design of IH that, whether intentionally or not, create an environment that fosters cross-cultural communication'. He saw the size and shape of the tables in the dining room as being of particular importance in a residence where the rent included three meals a day. This virtually ensured that most residents went down to the dining room for most meals and the tables for eight to ten people appeared to be ideal for encouraging conversation:

> The round shape of the tables maintains everyone at a reasonable distance from everyone else for holding a conversation, and assigns an equal status to anyone sitting at the table … with more people sitting at a table, it would be more common to have multiple conversations going on at the same time at the same table … creating a lot of noise and dividing the people sitting at the table into subgroups.

According to Andrés, a record set in 1995, illustrated in the previous chapter, showed that, in fact, seventeen-and-a-half people could be squeezed around one table (the half being the baby daughter of the Chens from South Korea who were living in the Maze units). The foyer couch, introduced in 1996, was the second important design feature he noted: 'comfortable, the right size and in a key location which most people would pass through during the day, and when tea and coffee trolleys were set up in the same location it only made things better.' The round poufs doubled as a table for playing Mah Jong and the whole area became a popular 'procrastinating centre', particularly around examination time. Finally, a third important design feature (and perhaps the most recent), was the phone system, 'with its voice mail, conference calling, message forwarding and other facilities, and the fact that it's all for free when making internal calls'. Later another resident was to remark: 'Internet access was once free at IH. Yes, it was Paradise!'

At the Food Fair held in May 2000, a discordant note struck the prevailing cross-cultural harmony — Taiwanese residents walked out after the Director told them to remove the Taiwanese flag from their booth. Following an incident the previous year, Sydney University and International House rules no longer permitted the display of Taiwan's political flag at the same time as that of the People's Republic of China. The residents were not mollified by the information that a cultural flag, known as the Chinese Taipei flag, was permitted, and the matter reached the national newspapers. Sydney University Vice-Chancellor, Gavin Brown, was asked to make a ruling after what, according to Department of Foreign Affairs sources, was a 'rare incident at an Australian university'. A diplomatic source put this unusual event down to 'a resurgence of Taiwanese pride after the recent pro-independence victory', but diplomacy in the House, led by the Director and a remarkable Chair of IHMA, Juan Camilo Reyes Hernandez, ensured that there was no recurrence in 2001.

In the first Alumni Newsletter for 2000, Toshiko Mori, the President of SUIHAA, reported 'a rewarding and enjoyable experience last year'. After Pauline (Seaich) Kennedy left the House in 1993, Gwen (Burrows) Ng, the very active Secretary of the SUIHAA Executive Committee, and later Toshiko herself, became peripatetic: they literally carried their office on their backs, both upstairs and down. However, in early 1999 they had been allocated an Alumni Office; documents could now be filed and serve as accessible reference material and, as a result, it was possible to list a large number of alumni who had not been receiving the Alumni Newsletters. The completion of the Alumni database by Toshiko and the website designed by her husband, Youngsok Song, officially launched in March 1998, proved to be sufficiently functional to search for friends and promote communication, so that within two years the number of visitors to the association's website had already exceeded 6,000.

Early in the year SUIHAA had been informed about intending visitors to Sydney during the Olympic Games and this led to a reunion lunch, which was held at International House on Sunday, 10 September, just before the start of the Games. The suggestion by Michael Brown, who was coming from Canada to attend the Games, was taken up by an alumna of his time, Fiona McEachern, and developed into a memorable occasion. The lunch was attended by more than 130 people (some with their children) and included not only alumni, but also members of Council, International House Fellows and former members of the Women's Committee whose organisation and personal assistance had helped so much in the early days of the House. Toshiko was thrilled to discover that each year of IH history, from 1967 to 2000, was represented by at least one former resident. The goodwill among those former residents and staff was expressed, both at the lunch and directly to Ruth Shatford, by donations towards significant improvements to the Log Cabin in Belanglo and the proposed rooftop leisure centre that was still awaiting local council approval.

During the Games, Sydney itself resonated goodwill and enthusiasm. Visitors were welcomed by countless numbers of volunteers, strangers talked freely to each other and there was a general feeling that it might at last be possible even for warring nations to live together in peace.

But that was in 2000...

The following year a 'Briefing and Planning Day' was organised for 10 March with the intention of re-visiting the Langley Committee Report of 1980, which had made recommendations 'concerning the fabric, purpose and administration of the House for the 1980s'. Though in 21 years much had changed, Council felt it should 'try to recast many of its suggestions and recommendations within the current context'.

David Shannon, a member of Council, conducted the day-long workshop held at the Seymour Centre and those invited included not only members of Council but also representatives of residents, staff and alumni. It was interesting to look around the table and note that, of the 26 people in attendance, no fewer than thirteen had at some time been resident in the House. Ruth Shatford detailed her concerns about the fabric and upkeep of the House and there were suggestions for possible future action, such as one relating to a survey of residents to establish what they saw as desirable facilities and, importantly, to discover what fee increases the residents thought they could sustain to provide such facilities.

For the residents, the new year began in style, on the annual Harbour cruise where, to quote Juan Camilo Reyes Hernandez, the new Chair of IHMA, 'imported Latin-American music gave the night a special exotic touch'. As another resident described it, 'As the boat broke through the waves, it also broke the ice between us ...' For many who came from overseas to International House, the House was their first real experience of Australia, what Benjamin Tupman would later describe as 'a totally alien country'. But, in his view, 'even for Australians, coming to IH could cause culture shock: you're entering a new place with new rules. There are people there who already know them: scary people who know exactly where the paper cups are kept and how to get the lift working if it gets stuck between floors...' But halfway through the year, just after he had left, the lift that he characterised as 'possessed by Satan himself … regularly skipped floors, got stuck in between, free fell and generally made you hope that you had an up-to-date will when you boarded it', had been replaced by a reliable electronic version.

One area still under-utilised at this time was the roof area of the main building. As mentioned in the first chapter, early plans for 'a charming rooftop apartment and garden for the Assistant Director' had been abandoned when it was learned that the addition of one more floor would mean installing a sprinkler system. Time would show that there was once a fire alarm in IH that was the result of a real fire, but given the number of false alarms from such disparate causes as burning toast and, it is recorded, a 'sudden blow from the poorly executed swing of a samurai sword', the management's fears of generations of soaked residents with sodden bedding and books were obviously based on a foreseeable reality.

However, Ruth Shatford's plan for a rooftop leisure centre was not restricted by these regulations. Work begun at the end of 2000 was completed with no loss of the spectacular views of Sydney University, the city and the Harbour Bridge. Filling the open bays with safety glass had increased the safety of the area as well as providing a windbreak; a large barbecue was connected to the main gas line and a stainless steel sink plumbed in beside it. Clotheslines were retained at the Glebe end and at the Redfern end a large shade-cloth structure and two market-place umbrellas gave shelter from the weather. Teakwood outdoor furniture had been purchased and well-advanced potted shrubs, the gift of a visiting Japanese alumna, completed this excellent outdoor addition to recreational areas in the House.

The Log Cabin in Belanglo State Forest also benefited from the generosity of three anonymous alumni: SUIHAA hosted a 'Stargazing Evening and Barbecue' there on 4 August as a welcome for new residents and when a large busload of them arrived they were pleased to find Brian Farmer ready to lead familiarisation tours of the Log Cabin site as well as kangaroo-spotting expeditions along the forest roads. As night fell, members of the Macarthur Astronomical Society generously set up their telescopes and willingly shared them and their expertise with many fascinated residents. Roger Wescombe summed up the occasion in the next SUIHAA Newsletter and particularly noticed the very welcome improvements:

> The Log Cabin is in great shape these days. The sound and smell of the pine forest, the carpet of pine needles to walk on, the crisp air, the clear sky with its blaze of stars …

these things haven't changed. But now the visitor, whether adventurer, sportsperson or poet, can also be comfortable. Alumni who haven't visited the cabin for some years will be pleased to find that the toilets are now adjacent to the bathrooms instead of out in the mulga; the ceiling lining now keeps the bats out so that you no longer feel that you are on a set of a Dracula movie; and there's enough hot and cold running water for normal use. Those who joined this splendid event were fortunate indeed.

With such a mature-age group of residents (age range 18–59, median age 25), it had been apparent for some time that support from a formally appointed Program Director was no longer required, and when Jill McRae retired in 1999 she was not replaced. A greatly increased number of IHMA Committee members — there were now some fifteen of them — ensured a vigorous program of well-organised events. These began in Orientation Week, complemented by SUIHAA's Calendarfest welcome to new residents, and continued throughout the year. The aim was to set up as many activities as the IHMA and International House budgets allowed, and they ranged from the formal Flag Dinner and the Food Fair through less organised events, such as the Inter-floor Games, both indoor and outdoor, salsa and jazz dancing lessons as well as, this current year, weekly Spanish and Arabic lessons. There were disco nights, rooftop barbecues and parties and the 'Assassination Game' so graphically described by Brendon Drain, which, to quote the IHMA Yearbook, 'allowed residents, especially new ones, to integrate into the community'! There were somewhat more cultural events, such as a trip in the House bus to Canberra's National Gallery for the exhibition of Frida Kahlo and Diego Rivera's Mexican paintings, which particularly interested the 'Latino' group in the House, and invitations to speakers to discuss world issues — so much was happening that it must have been hard at times to fit in essential study.

In many ways this level of community events meant that matters in the great world beyond the House had minimal impact: there was little discussion about the 'Tampa' incident in August, when a Norwegian ship's captain, Arne Rinnen, followed the rules of the sea and rescued Afghan refugees from their sinking ship; even less awareness of a Cabinet meeting on 29 August that passed retrospective legislation on 'border control' to prevent these 'illegal immigrants' landing on Christmas Island, thereby triggering a chain of events that would lead to the controversial 'Pacific solution' centred on forced incarceration on

Nauru, among other places. This innocence of the impact of international disasters was soon to change.

On 11 September 2001 (a date forever after to be known as '9/11' without further description), terrorists crashed planes into the World Trade Center Twin Towers in New York and the Pentagon in Washington. Among the residents there was a particular empathy for those Americans living in the House — and a fear of what the future held for them themselves, particularly for those far from home, as they lived with the daily reality of the terror that not only 'flieth by night' but by day as well.

Ruth Shatford wrote immediately to the International Houses of New York and Washington to express, on behalf of IH Sydney, 'our heartfelt sympathy and the assurance of our continuing kindest thoughts'. Messages of concern and support were received from many other International Houses worldwide and Donald Cuneo, President of the New York House, said that 'their words, reaffirming the principles for which International House stands, have calmed and boosted our spirits'.

On Friday 14 September, here in Sydney, we had the privilege of hearing Truong Mealy, a distinguished alumnus from Cambodia and a former Cambodian Ambassador to Japan, speak at a formal dinner in the House to very subdued residents who were still trying to come to terms with the reality of the horror that had struck the US and the news of the carnage in New York. Mealy, who had survived the enormity of the Cambodian tragedy and, following years of working as Secretary-General of the Association of Cambodians in France and for King Sihanouk as Director of the Royal Cabinet based in Thailand, after many years of exile from his own country, had become, in retirement, a 'Goodwill Ambassador' for Cambodia and 'La Chaîne de l'Espoir' ['The Link of Hope']. He spoke gently but impressively, to a very attentive audience, of the power of the individual to make a difference in the quest for peace, democracy and human rights.

In January 2002 it seemed that it would be just a normal year for the administration of International House — until the shock news of Ruth Shatford's early retirement for health reasons turned it into another transition year. As Director, Ruth Shatford had been tireless, not only in her devotion to her administrative work, but also in her interest in the residents' welfare, particularly in relation to the challenging task of providing food that was not only nutritious but acceptable to the different cultures and tastes represented in the House — an interesting and seemingly impossible goal. According to Agnes Fiamma, Food Co-ordinator for IHMA in 2001, her own role of fielding complaints made her feel akin to an agony aunt, but in the end, as a result of the Director's efforts and supported by the response of the caterers, she did learn that 'overall people think the food is not too bad, not too good' ... but as an instantly available topic of conversation, as other contributors here have observed, IH food was 'part of the glue that binds us all together'.

Ruth Shatford's directorship was also characterised by her efforts to improve facilities — the Rooftop Leisure Centre is an outstanding legacy — and improvements to the dining room included the addition of acoustic panels on the walls, which were later interspersed with the ethereal beauty of Mika Igarashi's paintings. But most important of all was her care and understanding of the unique community in her charge. As she herself wrote in the SUIHAA Newsletter just before she retired:

> It has been interesting for me to reflect on the House, its community and purpose, and on the role of the Director. It is crucial to understand that the best resources are to be found in the residents. You have to recognise that residents are academically able, have musical, artistic and sporting abilities, have the organisational and social skills and the maturity to be living on their own, away from home, pursuing high level studies and generally making a life for themselves. Most have deliberately chosen this environment to live in and have enormous good will towards the mission of the House and towards its community. The Director's role, in essence, is to enable residents to achieve their goals in a way that is not directive or intrusive ... At International House, the community is functioning well if the residents feel the Director is not needed. Being 'hands on' in this position oddly enough requires being hands off in practice!

All of us who had the privilege of knowing and working with Ruth viewed her departure with great regret, particularly as it was for medical reasons. But throughout the early months of the year — months of medical onslaughts — her cheerfulness and lively sense of humour never deserted her and many new residents would have been completely unaware of anything amiss. With her departure imminent, the search was now on for a new director ...

After advertising widely, receiving no fewer than 41 applications and interviewing several candidates, the Council of International House decided that the applicant they felt most able to follow Ruth in this important role was the current Assistant Director, Jessica Carroll. When Jessica's appointment was announced in April, she was surprised and touched to come home to find flowers and cards on the doorstep of her Maze unit. 'I have to say that it took me by surprise, but it shouldn't have, since it expressed the well-known thoughtfulness of the residents of IH.'

She had been Assistant Director since April 2000, so had already had two years' experience in IH when she applied for the position of Director. As a registered psychologist with a Master's degree in psychology, she had had close connections with Sydney University since her first appointment in 1990 as Administrative Assistant in the Academic Appointments Unit, and most recently as Personnel Manager of the College of Humanities and Social Sciences. But this just gives a bare outline of her competencies, so I was very pleased that she agreed to subject herself to yet another interview.

'Fire away with the questions, then', said Jessica when I confronted her with my tape recorder in her office, obviously remembering some of the curly ones thrown at her by the Council's Selection Committee. 'This isn't an interrogation', I protested. 'Just tell me a little about yourself.' So she did. Jessica is Irish and was born in a working-class suburb in Dublin. Both her parents were also born in Dublin and her mother had to leave school at thirteen to help take care of her three siblings. At fifteen, on the death of her mother, she worked in a laundry to help with family expenses and it was there that she met her husband, Jessica's father. One of eight children, he also left school at an early age and Jessica has a vivid memory of his story of walking five miles to school, bare foot and carrying a sod of turf for the school fire.

Her parents met at a 'laundry social' dance in their teens and their first home was a dilapidated rented flat in the inner city. Her father, a self-taught motor mechanic who built cars for British Leyland, scraped together 50 pounds for a deposit on their first house and when the first baby was born she was cradled in the bottom drawer of their chest of drawers. Jessica, born two years later, attended local convent schools where her chief interest was sport — specifically basketball — and, at the age of eighteen, she went to New York on a basketball exchange program. She graduated from high school in 1984, the first member of her family to do so, and worked for four years as a computer accounts officer.

Economically, Ireland in the 1980s was still very depressed and, for the young Irish, emigration seemed to be the way of the future.

When I asked her why she chose Australia, she said, 'I had been to New York and London but sunny Australia, as presented on television in *Neighbours,* seemed to be the most exotic destination!'

She arrived in Sydney in 1988, knowing only one friend, and found a casual secretarial job almost immediately. This was followed by a casual appointment at Sydney University and then a permanent one. She applied to do an Arts degree part-time, her Masters in psychology followed and during this time she also became an Australian citizen. After six years of study, two years' work experience in the Centre of Education and Research into Ageing, and registration as a psychologist, she returned to Human Resources at Sydney University.

Apart from her academic achievements and strong links with the University, Jessica feels that her personal story gives her a real affinity with many residents of IH. As a young person she, too, moved far away from the land of her birth, her family and everything that was familiar, and this was sadly brought home to her by her mother's sudden death in Ireland a few years ago. As she said about her family, 'You always worry about them and they about you'. But as the new Director of International House, she committed herself to 'build on and strengthen the current positive and vibrant sense of community in the House'.

A whirlwind of change blew throughout the House in 2002. As the new Director had previously been the Assistant Director, another appointment had to be made. Once again, after formally advertising the position and interviewing a number of applicants, the Selection Committee decided to look nearer home. A Senior Resident, Giselle Manalo, who had not actually applied for it, was offered the position. At the end of the year she described her two years at IH — as resident, Senior Resident and then Assistant Director — as a 'roller coaster ride', into which she had also fitted a Masters course in International Public Health and carved out a new professional career in Sydney. The changes did not stop there.

As was customary, there was now a new Chair of IHMA, Michelle Chalmers, the only Australian-born resident to hold that position in the first seven years of this decade — in spite of some early concerns at the inception of the association that language difficulties would deter overseas students from participating in meetings or being on the executive committee.

All four Senior Residents were new to their positions and there was an almost complete turnover of staff in the IH office. The previous year, 2001, had proved to be a challenging one, not least because of the recently introduced Goods and Services Tax (GST) being applied to certain services provided by university colleges and halls of residence. In order to comply with the new requirements, Council decided to upgrade the Business Manager's position to assist the Director with the new problems. The House was fortunate indeed that Beverley Fox, very experienced in residential college management after eighteen years at Dunmore Lang College, Macquarie University, was prepared to take the position in April 2002. Carla Bekker (Silva), Personal Assistant to the Director, then left to pursue the academic interests with which Ruth Shatford had given her so much encouragement, and Claudia Morales was appointed to replace her.

For Claudia, however, this was a return to familiar territory: arriving from Chile with her family in 1984, she attended school in Sydney and after completing a secretarial course in 1989 she was appointed to the position of receptionist at International House. She later became secretary to the Director, Geoffrey Andrews, then Acting Bursar during the Bursar's long service leave and during this time she enrolled in an Arts degree in Modern Languages at the University of New South Wales. In 1994 she met her husband, Alex Morales, during his brief stay in the House and left the House when they married in November of that year.

In 2002, after having three children, finishing her degree and obtaining national accreditation for interpreting and translation in Spanish and English, an IH alumnus, Pedro Borges, told her of the

Claudia Morales (Soto-Ferreira), Personal Assistant to the Director, 2006

position of Personal Assistant to the Director that was available at International House. With Claudia's six years' previous experience in the House, her appointment at this time was to prove invaluable.

Throughout all these changes a remarkable degree of stability was provided by the presence of Michael Farrugia, building manager since 1996, and Fiona Gallop, in charge of housekeeping services since 1998. The long-serving domestic staff — Sasha Chen, Ana Cumming, Erlinda Kiffin, Dubravka Knezevic, Lionel Ingram and, of course, Kaye Lynch, a member of the staff since 1981 — have between them successfully kept the House clean and polished right up to the present day. When I asked Kaye what had persuaded her to stay for an incredible 25 years, she put her loyalty down to the 'friendly and pleasant atmosphere' created by the students, and the amazing warm welcome she had received from Graeme de Graaff on her arrival in the House: 'Quite exceptional for somebody in the position I had applied for.'

Many of the House activities followed the regular pattern of previous years, with the annual Flag Dinner and Candlelight Ceremony and Dinner marking the beginning and the end of the academic year, and linking International House Sydney to International Houses throughout the world. This year's most significant innovation, the brainchild of IHMA Secretary, Vincent Malayapillay, was a Charity Sleepover. The Wool Room became an adult playground for indoor cricket, homemade Twister, Mah Jong and Trivial Pursuit. Five brave residents, including one woman — Nikki Norris — shaved their heads for substantial donations to the cause, and almost $1,800 was raised (with backing from IH and SUIHAA) for Children's Cancer Research.

The stargazing and barbecue welcome for the second semester's new residents was notable that year for the arrival of a busload of 40 residents at the Belanglo Log Cabin at 4 pm, only to find that the keys to the cabin had been left behind at the House. Frantic telephone calls to Giselle Manalo, the Assistant Director, resulted in arrangements for a second group to take the keys in the House bus to their stranded friends in Belanglo State Forest. There the whole affair had turned into a survival mission as residents and alumni alike joined in collecting wood for a huge bonfire — absolutely essential to protect some very inadequately clad residents from the bitterly cold winter's night. That done, barbecuing for nearly fifty people with forked twigs as their only utensils tested the ingenuity of the cooks. Under the expert supervision of the very experienced Richard Ng, they rose valiantly to the occasion — when Shatal Thapa, with his Swiss Army knife, had finally managed to prise the meat from the thick moulded-on plastic that encased it.

Fortunately the toilets were still accessible, but there was great relief when the residents travelling in the House bus, having inadvertently taken the scenic route via Wollongong, finally arrived four hours later with the keys. It might not be too far-fetched to see the whole affair as symptomatic of the effect of the excessive recent changes.

At the end of November an attempt was made to set up a new tradition: to have the Alumni Association's Annual General Meeting and barbecue in the rooftop garden. The location seemed ideal and the alumni were treated to city views, sunshine, wine and a buffet lunch prepared by the House's popular chef, Alex Chiam. But the tradition was fated to lapse in 2004, when the 40-degree temperature on the roof severely tested Chef Muan Hee Foo's stamina as he valiantly continued to barbecue, unprotected from the sun; the heat finally drove the whole exhausted and dehydrated company down to the air-conditioned comfort of the Wool Room.

As the first Alumni Newsletter went to press in March 2003, it was impossible to ignore concerns about the world situation; it was almost unbelievable that we had to acknowledge that Australia itself was at war. This war with Iraq, the first time in history that Australia had become a participant in a pre-emptive strike, caused deep divisions within the country. But not, apparently, in International House, although many residents far from home would inevitably be concerned about the safety of family and friends. On the contrary, the House appeared to have recovered the vitality that had, at times, seemed to be missing in the previous year.

The new Chair of IHMA, Jill Gambill from the USA, reported: 'The academic year of 2003 began with a bang, with almost half of IH consisting of incoming new residents. The energy and excitement level they brought was incredible!' Sports became a huge part of House life in the first semester. IH teams participated in basketball and soccer tournaments; and cricket, badminton and tennis were played regularly. The Food Fair, a paintball skirmish and a chess tournament were 'in the works' and the IH shop was completely revamped with fresh paint, beanbags and a café-like atmosphere.

At a special luncheon on Saturday, 21 June, SUIHAA was delighted to honour Ian Hudson, an Honorary Fellow of Sydney University and longstanding benefactor and Fellow of International House. He is the only member still living of that group of Rotarians who formed the original Fund Raising Committee for International House and he was the driving force of the enterprise. As Graeme de Graaff put it, he has remained 'generous with his time, his wisdom, his contacts and his purse' ever since.

Honouring Ian Hudson, 2003; l to r: Jessica Carroll, Director,
Graeme de Graaff, Lauris Elms, Ian Hudson, Sheila Hudson, Brian Farmer,
Phillip Milton

At the lunch, attended by people whom Ian had touched over a long period, Brian Farmer, distinguished alumnus, was able to make a fascinating presentation, in the style of 'This is your Life', to Ian and his wife, Sheila. From Brian's well-researched speech, guests heard of just some instances of Ian's philanthropy and services to a wide number of communities. From Evanston, Illinois, a message of congratulations was received from Bhichai Raatakul, World President of Rotary; and Sarnie Hay, the current President of the Rydalmere Rotary Club, which Ian had joined as a charter member in 1955, spoke of Ian as 'a man who is not just a Rotarian but someone who has made this the kind of world in which we want to live. Ian's contributions at home and in the far corners of the world, are a contribution of the heart that cannot be quantified in words. His is a contribution counted in lives saved and people changed'.

Ian Hudson's service to Sydney University's International House extended from 1962 to 1995, but his interests and influence were not merely local: he led the Rotary contingent that supported villages for abandoned children in Europe; he raised large sums of money, as well as making substantial personal donations, to Rotary's PolioPlus campaign to rid the world of polio and, when there was early resistance to the Youth Exchange Program with Japan, he travelled to Tokyo at his own expense to sort out the problems with Japan's Rotary leaders.

Ian and Sheila Hudson with the first four Directors of the House, 2003; l to r:
Geoffrey Andrews, Ruth Shatford, Ian Hudson, Jessica Carroll,
Sheila Hudson, Graeme de Graaff

Early business connections, which saw him travelling to Thailand, developed into a true friendship with the Thai people and those he touched ranged from mountain people in the north (for whom he tried to find viable economic alternatives to the growing of the opium poppy) to communities in Thailand that benefited from the schools and hospitals he helped to develop and, as the Thai Consul General in Australia, he gave direct personal help to His Royal Highness the Crown Prince of Thailand on his visits to Australia. In recognition of Ian's valuable services to the Thai people, His Majesty the King of Thailand bestowed on him the award of Commander of the Most Noble Order of the Crown of Thailand, the highest decoration that may be granted to a foreigner. A former Thai Ambassador to Australia, Padung Padamasank, sent a personal message of thanks from Bangkok to Ian on this special occasion.

Finally, there was a tribute from Phil Wilson, the Appeals Director of the Salvation Army, which Ian had supported since his service in the south-west Pacific area during the Second World War. He had perceived then that 'It was only the Salvos that cared about us. I was determined — if I got out of there — that I was going to help these people'. And over the years he had honoured his promise in many ways.

After the many awards bestowed on him, Sydney University International House and its Alumni honoured Ian Hudson especially for his service to the House; for his significant contribution to the development of the Log Cabin at Belanglo; to the alumni and to his continued moral and financial support to the residents of the House, particularly through the Ian Hudson Scholarship. Brian Farmer concluded his presentation by saying: 'Ian is an extraordinary man and we are all the better for having been touched by him.'

Ian Hudson's involvement with the building of the Log Cabin has been acknowledged earlier. It was there, in the second semester of 2003, that a 'massive turnout' of excited residents at the Belanglo stargazing event were rewarded by a glimpse of Mars, visible to the naked eye as it climbed slowly above the trees on a perfect starry night, although only the two residents from Norway glowed in the arctic weather.

Now in its second year, the Charity Sleepover seemed set to become an IH institution. Residents, and even the Director, enthusiastically dyed their hair bright colours — or even shaved it for the right price — and allowed themselves to be auctioned off as 'servants for the day'. With donations from International House and SUIHAA, the significant amount of $4,500 was raised for UNICEF.

It looked as if the following year would benefit greatly from the activities of this IHMA, and particularly its Executive Committee. Craig Prebble, the Secretary, and Avis Ying, the Treasurer, worked tirelessly with Jill Gambill 'to strengthen interactions with the University of Sydney Union, restructure the IHMA accounting procedures' and generally to organise and document their combined knowledge for the following year's committee. As a result, IHMA was shortlisted, for the first time, for the Excellence Award by the University of Sydney, an award that acknowledges the best clubs and societies at the University.

However, according to Christopher Clarke, the newly elected Chair of IHMA who describes himself as 'Chilean British', 2004 'seemed to start slow' and only gradually picked up speed: 'Older residents have shrunk as they found themselves lost amidst the new... intimidated by the majority.' It was certainly apparent that, with temporary exchange students from the USA and elsewhere, the increasing number of residents enrolled for a single semester was overtaking the number of those staying for longer periods and this required adjustment on all sides. As all had to enrol at Sydney University, in many ways it simply reflected University demographics and this pattern seemed set to continue. Yet, as Chris reported, 'the mingling has already begun, and as we have slowly found out, the Canadian medical students seem to be overtaking IH'.

The new committee was duly elected and interesting ideas and plans came out of it. At the Bronte Beach barbecue the Canadian medical students proved their worth by assuming the cooking duties when the majority of others were 'too preoccupied with the surf'. At a well-organised Flag Dinner, Dionigi Gerace, an entertaining Italian, made a remarkable impression not only at the dinner, when he insisted on dressing in Pakistani clothes to demonstrate the multicultural aspect of IH, but also during his entire single semester in the House.

The Director, Jessica Carroll, married Phillip Milton on 29 May 2004 and, in spite of her attempts to keep this significant change in her life low-key, IHMA and SUIHAA felt that the occasion should be marked. They combined to express their congratulations and good wishes for the future by supplying an enormous wedding cake, sufficient to be shared by all at the annual IH Food Fair, just prior to the wedding.

Following this, Jessica flew to London to attend the International Houses' Worldwide Conference, hosted by London International Student House, and she was introduced to HRH Princess Anne at a garden party held in Regent's Park. She later reported that the conference was a great success, with twelve International Houses from around the globe represented. The most significant themes discussed concerned ways of fostering communities where students and scholars from all corners of the world could live in harmony while learning lessons of international understanding and fellowship.

In the semester break in early July, Chris Clarke and Rima Rached attended the National Association of Australian Universities and Colleges (NAAUC) in Perth. Chris was later to report that he saw Sydney International House as 'unique': the fact that IH still had a preponderance of postgraduates and an average age of 24 created the difference. As a result he found it 'exceptionally hard' to find there ideas and issues that were relevant to IH. Throughout the week the main subjects of almost every conversation, lecture and discussion group centred around alcohol and 'freshers'. In his personal opinion the first was not an issue at IH and the second did not even exist. Like Emily Christie who reported on the NAAUC conference in 2003, one major difference between IH and the other colleges was the absence of extreme initiation ceremonies. In her report, she addressed some comments to her IH readers:

> Next time you start complaining that it's too cold on the roof for a barbecue, or that you have to be nice for a whole week to someone you've never seen before, just remember that we're not asking you to take an egg out on a date or to stand in buckets of regurgitated matter. More importantly, we're not asking you to drop your trousers every time you

hear 'Eagle Rock', a tradition which is apparently strictly followed in colleges around the nation.

One idea that Chris did approve was the simple one of getting to know people and what they are passionate about, 'for it addressed the problem of the big turnover and short stays' that now characterised the frequently changing population of IH. However, he came to the conclusion that the House should seriously consider whether its future membership of NAAUC was, in fact, essential.

The second semester saw a review of the IH Library completed and the implementation of various recommendations began. Meanwhile from Athens, Fani Manikakis-Nicolaidis sent news of her work as a volunteer at the Athens Olympics with her houseguest, Rebecca Lamb, the daughter of Belinda. Fani wrote to 'all past and present residents of all longitudes and latitudes: "Faithful to the ideals of IH, we are here as volunteers and send cordial greetings of friendship, peace, tolerance, brotherhood and international understanding from the birthplace of the Olympic Games, Athens"… with much love, Olympic spirit and the light of brotherhood from Greece'.

In spite of being eloquently described as a 'Frankenstein' by Daniel Ackland — a very senior Senior Resident and a second-generation member of IH — International Night, as usual, went off with great éclat. On this occasion SUIHAA made one of their own rare contributions to I-Night and the audience was treated to an explosion of 'SUIHAA Night Fever' in a return to the seventies, with jive, rock'n'roll, the Cha Cha and the Twist, choreographed by the talented Assistant Director, Giselle Manalo, and performed by energetic SUIHAA committee members of that vintage.

In October, with fund-raising for a proposed *History of International House* getting under way, Nuli Lemoh, the President of SUIHAA, organised an African Cultural Night to support and advertise the project. Members of the Sierra Leone community, ably assisted by Nuli himself and the Sierra Leone Cultural Dance Group — eight 11- and 12-year-old girls of inexhaustible energy — gave a demonstration of 'Talking Drums' and a lively display of traditional dances, highlighted by a fearsome, masked devil.

The end of 2004 was marked by the devastation of the Boxing Day tsunami that literally engulfed huge areas of the coasts of South-east Asia, Sri Lanka and India. Daily reports presented the ever-increasing magnitude of this catastrophe, which saw families, friends and neighbours changed forever by the loss of loved ones and the destruction of homes and workplaces. Destroyed communities faced the challenge of rebuilding not only their homes, towns and cities but also their lives.

Flurries of emails passed between IH residents and alumni as friends enquired anxiously about those known to be living in affected areas; and one new resident, Vijayasarathi Ramanathan, was able to share his personal experiences of working as a Resident Medical Officer in Casualty in a hospital in Madras, just 500 metres away from the coast of Chennai, Tamil Nadu, in India. Within hours the hospital started to receive patients affected, directly and indirectly, by the tsunami, for although it was in an area where the shore was a long way from the centre of population, many of the worst injuries were due to accidents sustained as people fled in sheer terror. On the third post-tsunami day, while working in a medical camp in a nearby coastal district, the horrendous scenes of death and destruction that Vijay encountered remained etched in his memory and he could only derive a little comfort from the fact that he had been able to give some professional help.

As the start of the academic year drew near, Vinci Liu, the new Chair of IHMA, created the first ever Orientation Program to cover the phase before the official beginning of first and second semester. He had observed the huge turnover of residents in 2003 and had noted, like his predecessor Chris Clarke, that the influx of new residents in 2004 had made older residents feel seriously outnumbered. Vinci recognised the importance of first impressions:

> This initial interaction ... would probably determine how residents related to one another for a long time to come. Many new residents arrive two to three weeks before the beginning of the Semester and they have very little to do. It's kind of odd that we have all these residents around, free, and not meeting each other... This is the time that IHMA should mix things up... You can't make everyone be friends, but you should at least make sure that the opportunity is there.

And that is what he aimed to accomplish when he began the first 'Phase 1 Orientation Program' for each semester.

The IHMA Committee asked the House to provide free room and board for two 'Orientation Co-ordinators', who would volunteer their time, and also to supply a small budget for them. The scheme was then under way: new residents were introduced by old residents to the local amenities and to the city of Sydney itself, with organised trips to the Fish Markets, the Opera House Bar, with its spectacular views of the harbour and the Harbour Bridge, and the Opera House itself; there were visits to the cafes of Glebe and a Coogee to Bondi beach walk

— as well as very popular 'clubbing' in the CBD. Similar events were to prove popular in the second semester, ten days before the official 'Welcome Barbecue' on the IH rooftop and the longstanding, formal IH and Sydney University Orientation Programs. The details of both programs were meticulously documented and made available to the following year's IHMA Committee and, in the light of increasing rates of change, this well thought-out initiative appeared to be a very positive contribution to the welfare of the residents of the House.

The 2005 Food Fair, its usual delicious and unusual dishes concocted successfully with the bare minimum facilities available to the cooks from a wide number of different cultures, was not only enjoyed by the residents of the House and their guests, it also welcomed some very appreciative visitors from the International Houses of both the University of New South Wales and Newcastle University.

After the Chair of IHMA had remarked that it was absurd that the present residents had heard about almost everyone else except the indigenous people of Australia itself, the Director made contact with the Koori Centre (Sydney University) and arrangements were made for an Aboriginal cultural event. This was organised by the Thulli Dreaming Dance Group and the interest generated among the residents may well result in other events that could explore more aspects of indigenous culture and the history of Aboriginal kinship networks.

During 2005, two former International House Chairpersons were honoured. Mrs Daphne Kok was made a Fellow of the University of Sydney. She has had a long association with the House, having served for some years as the Senate representative on the IH Council, then as Chair in 2004 and 2005. She was also at different times Deputy Chancellor of Sydney University.

The second was Emeritus Professor Hans Freeman, who was created a Member of the Order of Australia for his services to science in the Queen's Birthday honours list. He was teaching in the Chemistry Department of the University of Sydney when International House was established in 1965 and as a member of the Sydney Chapter of the US International Houses had been party to that group's throwing its support behind the Sydney University IH project. By the time it was officially opened in 1967, the Senate had appointed him to the IH Council, on which he served actively for a quarter of a century, including a period as Chair. He was further involved in the House during the late eighties when he led the fund-raising drive for the project to modify the buildings.

At the end of the year, SUIHAA itself elected to propose a nominee for one of the rare Alumni Awards for Achievement, established to recognise a former resident who has made a significant contribution to society, to international, intercultural or interracial understanding and friendship. Also taken into account is the extent to which a nominee has been unrecognised or under-recognised for her or his achievement and contribution. The International House Council unanimously agreed that Dr Anne Walker (1970) should receive this honour.

The award recognised Anne Walker's outstanding work in the field of sexually transmitted diseases in Sydney and Glasgow for the past 36 years. In particular, SUIHAA and the Council were impressed by her dedication to the welfare of those from disadvantaged backgrounds in a medical field that is so vital and yet publicised so little. Professor Sidney Gray, an alumnus and a member of the IH Council, agreed to represent both SUIHAA and the Council and present the award to Dr Walker in person in the UK. The presentation was made at a ceremony held in Glasgow, Scotland, on 26 March 2006 and around 40 people were present — family, friends and colleagues — for a most enjoyable and memorable occasion.

In July 2005 the Director, Jessica Carroll, embarked on a year's maternity leave and her daughter, Hannah, was born on 22 July. Keith Smith took Jessica's place, as Acting Director. When I interviewed Keith at the House, I found someone who regarded himself as a true Australian. He described himself as 'a Bowral boy' whose immediate ancestors included a convict highwayman who ran one pub in the city and another in Parramatta. Another ancestor, a stonemason, came over from Scotland and was involved in the building of the Great Hall of Sydney University — one might almost say that, at IH, Keith Smith had come home. After his initial interview by Council, Jessica showed him around the House and, as he remarked, 'The moment I walked through the front door I felt the ethos and the friendliness that is the House'. He was to find the job easy, partly because of the excellent preparation for the handover that Jessica had done, but also because of his strong network in Sydney University and his current position as manager of the Camden Campus Properties Office. 'In fact', he said, 'I have been juggling budgets for twenty years'.

On 3 September 2005, after a lapse of a few years, the Foundation Day Lunch and Address was re-introduced, with Hugh Mackay, the renowned social observer and distinguished writer, as guest speaker. Professor Richard Waterhouse also took the opportunity to launch the official appeal for funds to support the 'History of International House' publication project.

According to Vinci Liu, the Chair of IHMA, there was an ecstatic feeling among many residents after I-Night that year. It had been a great accomplishment by all participants, both on and off stage, when new talents emerged and new friendships were formed in the course of putting on sixteen different acts. Nehal Kapadia, one of the Social Co-ordinators, did an amazing job in organising and co-ordinating a very sophisticated show — not only on stage and backstage, but also with sound, lighting and technical crews, as well as the production of a video. But for the audience perhaps the most memorable performance was that of Jamie Bain's 'International House Academy of Dance'. With both of the first semester's dance instructors unavailable, Jamie Bain — one of IH's catering staff who just happened to be a professional dancer — was approached and, in spite of his already very full-time work, he volunteered to teach dance classes on Sundays and choreograph the exciting and very professional 'New Generation Dance' which delighted us all.

It was not surprising that after this success Nehal Kapadia was elected Chair of IHMA for 2006. Following the pattern for a 'Phase 1 Orientation Program' documented by Vinci Liu, she and her new IHMA Committee devised and carried through a similar one to engage the new residents during the same period. Once again, with an invitation to the Food Fair, she made sure that the link with University of New South Wales IH was maintained. Nehal put her own imprint on the House by electing an Environmental and Welfare Officer, following the water audit in the first semester; and the now well-established Charity Night was held as a 'Slave Auction' to raise funds for cancer research; it also became part of the brief of this new committee member.

In July, the Acting Director, Keith Smith, left the House and Jessica Carroll returned from maternity leave. The transition period was over.

The twelfth of August 2006 marked a memorable 39th Foundation Day Lunch and an entertaining address by the well-known broadcaster and member of Sydney University Senate, Adam Spencer. The fortieth anniversary of the founding of Sydney University's International House now hovers on the horizon and the Great Hall has been booked for the Foundation Day celebrations.

Sources

IH Archives:

Council of International House to the Senate, University of Sydney (1999–2004); Council House and Finance Meetings (1999–2005); Briefing and Planning Day (10 March 2001); Statistics of Residents (2000–2005); Tribute to Ian Hudson (21 June 2003) by Brian Farmer. IHMA Yearbooks 2000–2005; SUIHAA Newsletters 1999–2006 (volume 32, nos 1 and 2; volume 38, no 1)

Oral sources:

Interviews with Directors: Ruth Shatford in 1999 and 2006; Jessica Carroll in 2002 and 2006; with Keith Smith and Assistant Director Giselle Manalo in 2006. With IH office staff: Business Manager, Beverley Fox (2002–2006), and Personal Assistant to the Director, Claudia Morales (1989–1994, 2002–2006), in 2006; and with housekeeping staff: Fiona Gallop (1998–2006) and Kaye Lynch (1981–2006) also in 2006.

Interviews in 2006 also with IHMA Chairpersons: Christopher Clarke (2004), Vinci Liu (2005) and Nehal Kapadia (2006); and with SUIHAA committee member, Gwen Ng (1993–2006).

Publications:

The Australian, 'Taiwan Flag off the Menu', 31 May 2000

Truong Mealy, *Conquer our Destiny* (Hire-Tai Books, Japan. In International House library)

Chapter Seven

Overview

Richard Waterhouse

Both Rotary International and the International House movement had their origins in American Progressivism. The movement penetrated both major political parties, influencing the domestic and international policies of Presidents Theodore Roosevelt (1901–1908) and Woodrow Wilson (1912–1920). The political Progressives believed that science and efficiency should be the watchwords of reform and the means by which both rural and urban America were to be purged of corruption and made modern, democratic and humane. The more idealistic Progressives, led by Wilson, also believed that its principles were relevant and beneficial to countries other than the USA.

Yet, other Progressives distrusted both politicians and government institutions. Paul Harris, who founded the first Rotary Club in Chicago in 1905, decried what he saw as the corrupting influence of politics, and sought to make business and professional men ethical, responsible and committed to good works through infusing the Rotary movement with the ethos of 'service above self'. This commitment both to ethical business and professional practice and to community service became integral to the Rotary movement in Australia, which was founded in the interwar period. I suspect a Progressivism strongly tinged with Protestant Christianity inspired Harry Edmonds' vision to establish an International House in New York, although what allowed his dream to become reality was a good dose of nineteenth-century philanthropy, courtesy of John D. Rockefeller Jr.

At the time the University of Sydney International House was established, it was uncommon for wealthy businessmen or companies to fund major university projects, for it was a widely held Australian tenet that providing the finance for such things was a government responsibility. It is a sign of changing times that in recent years generous donations to the University have become more common, allowing for example, the establishment of a Centre for Security Studies and the United States Study Centre, although the latter was 'kicked off' with a generous initial grant from the federal government.

In the 1960s, Australian society was in a period of transition. The arrival of large numbers of post-war immigrants from Europe, many of whom were not of Anglo-Celtic origins, combined with the British government's decision to apply for membership of the European

Common Market, loosened the nation's economic, diplomatic and cultural ties to the UK, and threatened our accepted role as a European outpost on the fringes of Asia. But neither the Australian government, nor its people, were yet ready to accept the desirability of strengthening political and cultural ties with Asia. When the Colombo Plan was adopted by British Commonwealth nations in 1950, Australia was a willing participant, welcoming, in particular, students from Malaya and Indonesia. The Colombo Plan was designed to inhibit the appeal of Communism and, in the view of Australian authorities, the two above-listed nations were particularly vulnerable to the totalitarian left. Implementation of the Colombo Plan and the admission of increasing numbers of private students from Asia were also measures designed to blunt criticism of the White Australia policy, although the strictures that emanated from nations like India indicated pretty clearly the failure of this strategy. In any case Australia's Asian 'engagement' was driven by a misplaced sense of realpolitik.

In fact, the Colombo Plan succeeded in ways that were unintended and unwelcome as far as the Australian government was concerned. For the presence both of Colombo Plan and private students from Asia stirred Australian students, led by the SRC at the University of Sydney, to campaign against the White Australia policy, in the process forming alliances with people like the legendary Billy Lieu, a long-time campaigner against the Immigration Restriction Act. The Colombo Plan heightened the consciousness of Australian students in relation to Asia and it is in this context that the unsuccessful attempt by the Sydney University SRC in the 1950s to raise funds for the establishment of an International House on campus must be seen.

The cultural and political influence of the United States on Australia has a long history, extending back to the earliest years of European settlement. However, as British cultural influence declined in the 1950s and 1960s, so the vacuum was partly filled by American (popular) culture in the form of rock n' roll, films, television programs, and that institution that epitomised counter-cultural hedonism, the Californian surfing sub-culture — for it defied the work ethic, valorising instead the search for the perfect wave.

The period after the Second World War also saw a dramatic increase both in the membership and the number of Rotary clubs in Australia. The notion of service appealed to many business and professional men, in part, I suppose, because many of them had enlisted in the armed services during the Second World War. There they had learnt that service was both an obligation and a way of life. Perhaps, too, the notion of service connected easily to traditional Australian notions of mateship, in the process shedding mateship's radical rural and shearer connotations and providing it instead with a middle-class, urban respectability. Some intellectuals in the 1960s bemoaned the growing influence of the USA on Australia, voicing fears that we were in the process of becoming 'Austerica'.

Overall, however, Australians embraced American values and institutions because they seemed more democratic and forward-looking, more applicable to a former colony intent on engaging in the processes that would make it an independent nation than the values and institutions that were the vestiges of colonial dependence. In any case, the growing power and influence of Rotary in Australia, the willingness of the Rotarians in District 275 to commit themselves to the progressive vision of establishing International Houses both at the University of Sydney and the University of New South Wales, were testimony not only to the nation's determination to 'grow up' (a familiar cliché of the fifties and sixties) and engage in the wider world, but also of the positive influence of American culture on Australia.

In the aftermath of the *Murray Report* of 1957, the federal government committed itself both to expanding the Australian university system and providing greater access to undergraduate and postgraduate students through both undergraduate and postgraduate scholarships. Yet, despite this growth, there remained something highly traditional about attitudes to the function of universities in society, for the liberal ideal of the role of universities lived on. In the first place, the government accepted that an important role of universities was to provide a broad liberal education, not just a vocational one. In the second place, education was regarded as a right, not a privilege: universities were conceived as places of opportunity and, thus, as cornerstones of democracy. The federal government, therefore, accepted its responsibility to provide the overwhelming share of the funding to maintain and expand the tertiary sector.

In this context, universities were managed in informal ways and personal contacts were vital in getting things done. The relationship that Graeme de Graaff developed with Harold Maze was crucial in facilitating the building of International House and in establishing its institutions of governance. In the twenty-first century it is unimaginable that the staff de Graaff so carefully and skilfully recruited could be hired in the same informal and personal way. It is also inconceivable that such a project would proceed without a five-year strategic plan, a ten-year financial plan, showing an annual net return of at least fifteen per cent, and oversight by a committee chaired by the University's Chief Financial Officer. In an age when the University of Sydney now receives less than 30 per cent of its income from the federal government, the impetus towards becoming a corporate, profit-driven institution seems irreversible.

It is a truism to suggest that change and continuity have marked the forty-year history of International House at Sydney University. One constant source of complaint from decade to decade, as we have seen, relates to the quality of the food. Yet the widely shared dislike for IH cuisine had some fortunate consequences. In the early days, at least, some Australian students initiated the custom of inviting their overseas colleagues to their parents' homes. As a result, the latter were introduced to the delights, or otherwise, of baked Sunday dinners. In 1968, too, the practice of late night trips to Dixon Street was introduced. Two rules applied to these nocturnal journeys. First, only those who could fit in one car were able to make the journey (though this sometimes severely restricted numbers, because one of the conveyances used was a Morris Minor). Second, as noted in John Gascoigne's account of the seventies, one of the prospective diners had to be Chinese, because the preferred eating establishments were those connected to what we then termed gambling dens, with no menus in English. The formalisation of this cultural practice in the creation of the Supper Club in 1978, was a sign that the IH menu had not, apparently, improved over the decade.

Continuity was also reflected in the fact that a number of significant occasions were quickly established and have remained as the key events on the social and cultural calendar: these include the Flag Ceremony and Dinner, the Candlelight Ceremony and Dinner, House Dinners, International Night, the annual Ball and the Food Fair; and, in more recent years, the Inter-floor Games and the Charity Sleepover have become additions to the annual sequence. Those of us who attended the first International Night (which then encompassed the Food Fair) found it an unforgettable experience, for it revealed more obviously the richness and diversity of the cultures that were present in the House. Somehow, the attempts by the Australian residents to articulate an Australian culture through the reading and enacting of bush ballads and stories seemed inadequate in comparison with the Asian cultures on display, although these performances anticipated the revival of a Bush Legend nationalism that was to re-emerge in this country in the 1970s. For many of us raised on a narrow diet of overcooked Anglo-Celtic cuisine the (Asian) food also proved a revelation. In contrast, the Boston baked beans produced by Bob Kuzelka left some of us feeling in need of imminent hospitalisation. What is also significant about these major annual events is that for the most part they were conceived and organised by the residents themselves, evidence of the continuing policy of the Directors over the years to maintain a 'hands-off' approach, to allow the residents to organise and live their own lives.

One trope that runs continuously through the history of the House centres on the repeated attempts to develop outreach programs to the wider overseas student community – and their repeated failure. Such programs were attempted in the early de Graaff years and again during Geoffrey Andrews's tenure. They failed, as earlier chapters have shown, both because separate space resources were not available and because IH was specifically linked to the University of Sydney, which inhibited overseas students enrolled at other Sydney universities from availing themselves of the offered resources. But outreach had its uses. In the early days there was an impoverished medical student who could only afford to rent a room in a terrace on City Road. The terms of his lease prohibited him using the in-house toilet and bathroom facilities and so he became a non-resident member of International House for the specific purpose of gaining access to showers and toilets. In this instance the outreach program served a humane and practical, if not idealistic, purpose.

A sense of being different has also always marked the International House community. IH residents have always sought to distinguish themselves from the college community by claiming a higher degree of maturity and commitment to their studies and expressing a disdain for the rituals of initiation and the grog and sporting cultures that have marked some of the colleges. There is some truth in this, although their more recent policy of recruiting residents of both sexes has changed the ethos of the colleges. Many Sydney University academics look forward with pleasure to the annual faculty dinners sponsored by Wesley College, in particular. It is true that the introduction of the wine cellar at International House encouraged a responsible attitude to alcohol, but a dining culture emphasising a combination of wine, food and good conversation did not remain an IH monopoly. Moreover, students will be students, and some of the spontaneous Friday and Saturday night parties held in IH in the early days involved the consumption of copious amounts of alcohol. The capacity of one Australian economics postgraduate student for beer probably qualified him for membership of the Australian cricket team. And boys will be boys — despite the idealism and the commitment to brotherhood and sisterhood that pervaded the halls in the heady early days. On one occasion in 1968, a group of male college students tried to gatecrash an International House function. In response, the level 4 (male) residents turned a fire hose on them, proof perhaps that the larrikin tradition represented by Australian residents at International Night performances sometimes had real-life manifestations in IH culture as well.

For much of its history, the Women's Committee remained a fixture of IH life, its members indefatigable in raising funds for bursaries and amenities, as other writers here have acknowledged, as well as creating ties between the overseas students and Australian families. When I lived in IH, I did not think much about the contribution of the Women's Committee — although the shop seemed a wonderful convenience — but when I became a foreign student at Johns Hopkins University in Baltimore and benefited enormously from the host family scheme offered there, I came to appreciate the understated efforts of the Women's Committee in Sydney.

Similarly, the Alumni Association has played a vital role for most of the history of the House, its Newsletter not only reminding former residents of happy student days, but encouraging them to re-connect with lost IH friends; the Newsletter, too, has become a powerful public relations tool. And finally the continuing and enduring contributions of service-minded citizens like Ian Hudson and Brian Farmer are worthy of acknowledgement and remembrance. Their roles in the establishment of the Log Cabin and in the expansion of the House's accommodation are two examples of their hard work and dedication.

International Night, The Wool Room, 1975

Rotary's fund-raising role was vital to the establishment of International House and individual Rotarians and particular clubs have continued to assist in relation to matters of governance through their membership of the Council, as well as through fund-raising and outreach programs. But Rotary as a movement has moved into other fields of service. It is much less common now for a large group of clubs to unite in common endeavours. Rather, individual clubs have committed themselves both to international projects, such as the polio eradication program, and to specific local projects involving assistance to surf clubs, hospitals and nursing homes, and to those in the community who suffer from mental and physical disabilities. IH needs money for renovation and improvement, but it will need to develop new and innovative fund-raising processes.

Change is perhaps most clearly reflected in an altered ethos as the wide-eyed idealism of the sixties and seventies gave way to a more resident-focussed, a more pragmatic set of attitudes in subsequent decades; and in a shift in the characteristics of the student population. In large part inspired by the vision of Graeme de Graaff and Rosalie McCutcheon, many (albeit not all) of the early residents saw International House as something unique, a place to create an international community and to foster transcultural connections, and even a site that might contribute to the shaming of the White Australia policy. Today's students are necessarily more pragmatic: after all, a university education no longer guarantees employment and the costs of living are far greater, especially since the introduction of the mobile phone. The reasons for them to work hard at their studies and to engage in casual employment are compelling and they have little time to take up causes. In any case some of the main causes, such as the fight to end White Australia, are now ancient history.

When the House was founded, it will be recalled, the resident body was to comprise women and men in similar proportions to their numbers at Sydney University and to aim at equal numbers from Australia and overseas; preference in selection was to be given to advanced undergraduate and to postgraduate students. If at first there was difficulty in recruiting female residents, in later years it became — and still is — more and more of a challenge to attract Australian students generally. This matter, canvassed earlier, is also addressed in the following chapter, but I believe the decline may be attributable — in part at least — to rising costs and a culture in which students are more willing to live at home and spend their casual earnings on cars and phones, rather than on accommodation. It is disappointing to note, in particular, that the number of Australian women postgraduate students has declined significantly. Over the years residents have come from Hong Kong, Japan, Africa, Europe, North and South America, South and South-east Asia. Australia has contributed the greatest number of residents, although the combined numbers from Thailand, Indonesia and Malaysia are not far behind.

However, the decision by the federal government to treat tertiary education as an export industry and promote the recruitment of full-fee-paying overseas students, while at the same time reducing the size of government grants to universities — in the expectation that fees would make up the difference — has had a huge impact. Once, the federal government recruited overseas students (from South-east Asia in particular) both as an anti-communist tactic and as a palliative designed to limit the negative effects of the White Australia policy. Since the 1980s, overseas students have become essential to the economic well-being of Australian universities. At Sydney University, for instance, the Faculty of Economics and Business has relied increasingly on fee-paying undergraduate and postgraduate students from China. In contrast, the Faculty of Arts has benefited from the expansion of Study Abroad programs with United States universities; some of these students have spent their semester abroad as residents of IH, their short-term stays providing them with different experiences from those of longer-term residents.

A Belanglo Log Cabin group (Jessica Carroll, seated centre), c. 2004
(note Mollie Burns's solar hot water system on the roof)

And what does the future hold? First, it is likely that Sydney University will seek to attract an increasing number of overseas students from Asia, Europe and North America into fee-paying Master's programs. This offers the prospect of IH's recruiting postgraduate students likely to be resident for one or even two years. Second, the University will promote its short-term Summer and Winter School programs overseas, especially in North America and Europe, bringing in students who will perhaps enrol in only one or two units of study during their six-week stay. Such students offer the House both opportunities and challenges.

In 1849–1850, William Charles Wentworth led the movement that resulted in the founding of the first full colonial university in the second British Empire, the University of Sydney. There were two purposes: one purely educational, 'to enlighten the mind, to refine the soul of our fellow men', the other vocational, to train men to fill 'the high offices of state'. In the end, the role of the University of Sydney has far exceeded the one that Wentworth intended, for it enlightens the minds of women as well as men and it educates both Australian and overseas students not only to occupy 'the high offices of state' but also to occupy the high offices of business, science, medicine and, indeed, culture. In providing opportunities to men and women from a diverse range of countries and ethnic backgrounds, it has contributed to understanding and to democracy. And for its contribution to that process International House also has much of which to be proud.

Sources

My service as Head of the School of Philosophical and Historical Inquiry at the University of Sydney from 1999 to 2006 provided me with insights into the workings of the University and the directions of government and University policy. My understanding of Rotary and its changing purpose is based on my experience as a member of Gosford Rotary Club since 1999.

Publications:

Kenneth Cable, Clifford Turney, Ursula Bygott, *Australia's First: a Pictorial History of the University of Sydney 1850–1990* (Sydney, 1990)

Brian H. Fletcher, *Achieving for Others: the Rotary Club of Sydney, 1921–2005* (Sydney, 2005)

John Ritchie, *The Wentworths: Father and Son* (Melbourne, 1997)

Chapter Eight
The Future of International House: beyond 2007
Jessica Carroll, Denise North and David Shannon

It is appropriate when writing about the history of International House to give some thought to its future. In 2007, IH Sydney is poised to embark on the next major phase of its development. As with the birth of the International House project more than fifty years ago, growing demand for the right kind of on-campus accommodation, especially for international students, is one of the key circumstances that will drive this next phase of growth.

In that context, it is interesting to note the extent to which the core questions being asked at IH Sydney today are the same questions that have been asked since its beginning, and throughout its life. What is the minimum number of residents required for an economic operation? What is the appropriate allocation of limited space to various functions, notably bathrooms and kitchens, as opposed to group study areas? How should we resolve the tension between physical and social structures that promote community and those that facilitate independence? What should be the extent and nature of the House's role in the wider Sydney University community? And, most critically of all, where will the funds needed to realise the vision be found?

Over the forty years of the House's existence these key questions have been answered in different ways by the successive generations of the House's various guardians: members of Council, staff, residents and alumni. This history bears testimony to the way IH has adapted its core mission of promoting international fellowship to its changing social, cultural and economic environments. It is no surprise that today the House continues to face further changes in such environments.

Australian student life has changed considerably from the way things were in 1967 when the House opened. No longer are students exclusively students with the pursuit (an appropriately ambiguous word!) of their studies their full-time occupation. These days, students from the 'Y generation' have a broader network and many are also working, travelling, and socialising with their own group of friends. Their lives are busier than ever before. It is bewildering to see how they fit everything into their already crammed schedules but somehow they seem to thrive on 'student' life. Today, that life reflects the changes in society and technology over the last decade or so. Council and residents back in 1967 would have laughed at the thought of mobile phones, wireless computers, the Internet and e–learning, and students holding down one or even two part-time jobs.

The role of IH and the experience that it can offer have also changed since it opened. During the House's first decade there were about 700 international students in the University, and almost ten per cent of them lived in the House. Now there are approximately 8,700 international students, and the proportion living in IH is around two per cent. In the 1960s, an international focus was something quite different and special within the University. Today every faculty and college has international students and a program of recruiting from the international market. Australia has become much more multicultural and internationally aware. Experiences that were once special to IH can now be found in most classrooms and in many residential situations across the country.

In other ways, too, IH is less clearly differentiated than once it was from other parts of the University and especially other residential facilities. For example, when it opened IH was quite unusual in housing both male and female students. It also quite deliberately avoided the apparatus of supervision and of acting *in loco parentis*; at IH students were always treated as adults. Today, this is more the norm than the exception throughout the University. In keeping with its original design, IH is still slightly less expensive than most other Sydney University colleges, but there is now less of a difference in price and in the range and standards of service provided. All this means a rethinking of where IH is heading and the best means to achieve its enduring goal of fostering international understanding.

This is the fortieth year since the opening of the University of Sydney's International House building, which is now a dated mixture of architectural influences from the sixties, seventies and eighties at the corner of City Road and Cleveland Street, especially visible since the new ultra-modern School of Information Technologies building has gone up right next door.

Consequently, one of the major issues currently under discussion by the Council is refurbishment of the building and redevelopment of the site. The building has served its community well for four decades, but we now need to upgrade bedrooms, bathrooms and common areas and provide modern study facilities for students. Customer expectations have changed considerably. Many want better amenities and better physical accommodation, different accommodation packages, more flexible catering arrangements and higher standards of service; and they want all this within price constraints. Students still expect many of the things from communal living that they always have — making lifelong friends and having a good time among these — but now want to find new ways of connecting with the numerous communities to which they belong.

Food is still, and always will be, on the agenda. Residents continue to value the common dining experience; every meal provides an opportunity to sit at one of the round tables and chat with other residents. This is an easy, no-pressure way for people to get to know one another and it makes a strong contribution to international fellowship within the House. However, there is an increasing demand for self-catering facilities in the expectation of a more independent lifestyle, perhaps also at a lower cost.

The facilities must also satisfy the needs of people who occupy the rooms during university vacations, because the economics of the House are best served by maintaining full occupancy throughout the year. Ideally, the facilities offered to university visitors, conference delegates and others during vacations should command a higher price than students pay. The need to refurbish and upgrade the current facilities is particularly compelling in relation to the vacation trade.

There is a general consensus in Council that minor refurbishment of the House will not satisfy the needs of future students and vacation guests. To ensure that the House will be able to continue its important role for at least a further forty years, it will be necessary to undertake either a major refurbishment of the current building or redevelopment of the IH site. Either approach will involve a comprehensive planning and costing exercise. Exactly what facilities are needed to satisfy the requirements of future residents and what implications will all this have in relation to the composition of the future IH community?

The importance of addressing the issue of the building and its facilities is made more urgent by the need to make IH more accessible to those with disabilities. Less able-bodied residents cannot at present access essential facilities such as the computer lab, the library or the games rooms on the top floor of the Rotunda. International House at the University of Chicago is currently in its final phase of renovation of its Courtyard and is being completely rebuilt to be in compliance with the US Disability Act, which requires the removal of any architectural barriers to accessibility. Sydney University IH will need to adopt the same approach and renovate or rebuild the areas of the House that are not accessible to people with disabilities. For this reason alone, extensive modification or redevelopment of the Rotunda area of the House may be necessary.

Ideas currently under consideration by Council include a total refurbishment of the current residential areas; extension of the East and Elkin wings, possible new development of a second section of the House where the Rotunda now stands as a number of self-catered apartments for students and academics who require or prefer this type of accommodation; relocation of House facilities on the ground levels, with no barriers to accessibility; and a new main entrance from Maze Crescent.

A decline in applications in 2003, particularly from Australians, has raised questions concerning marketing. One reason assumed responsible for the decline is that International House is not unique in the way it once was, back in the 1960s and 1970s, when students came from overseas to live with Australians, affordable accommodation on or near campus was hard to find and tertiary education was free to all students. Many of the current Australian students have parents who were born overseas, Sydney University and the city of Sydney itself are diverse and multicultural places and all the residential colleges on campus now accept international students, albeit in smaller numbers than IH. Nonetheless, the House continues to fill each year with a vibrant and varied group of enthusiastic residents from many nations who carry on with the customs and traditions already in place.

*Daphne Kok and David Shannon, Deputy Chair
and Chair of Council, 2006*

International House continues to attract over 45 different nationalities each year, but local student numbers have not often met the original goal of 50 per cent: at present the proportion is more like 22 per cent. This recent low level of Australian applicants is thought to be largely due to economics. Back in the early years it was possible for many Australian students to meet the costs of living in the House from their government scholarship, supplemented by holiday employment and occasional financial help from family. Today most Australian students require part-time work during term to make ends meet. They find the cost of IH less affordable. Some also find that the dine-in catering arrangements and participation in IH activities do not fit well with their employment schedules. There is, in addition, a widespread misperception among local students that IH is only for international residents. All of this underlines the need for the House to increase Australian numbers and to attract more students from countries that are either not represented or have limited representation.

Throughout the life of the House and its many challenges there has always been a sense of a real international community, which is not something that other communities or even Sydney University residential colleges can claim. If one searched for a similar place in Sydney it is doubtful that you would find such a diverse mix of people, especially one that interacts and co-operates as well as the IH community. But community means different things to different people and there has been some discussion about how to encourage such a group to engage fully.

As this history testifies, the House has also struggled with programs and community outreach. Non-resident membership and programs have been unsuccessful in the past, as residents felt that the House was imposing events on them or that their privacy was being compromised. The program of activities and the events that the House and Residents' Association currently produce are quite adequate for the busy resident community, but if the House's mission is to reach out to the wider University community or beyond, it will have to think seriously about the needs and expectations of the target audience and how to fund the resources to develop such an outreach program if it is to have sustainable success. It will also have implications for the physical structure of the building, not least because of the need for a separate space for outside functions so that these will not intrude on the residents.

The simple act of putting people with different backgrounds together in an everyday living environment allows International House to reshape its residents. Since 1967, some 8,500 residents have returned to the world beyond IH. All of them have been touched by the House

The Director, Jessica Carroll, with
Helen Xin Liu, holder of the
Ian Hudson Scholarship, 2003

in some way, hopefully in a positive way; and many have gone on to very successful careers in different academic and professional fields. Such alumni provide a considerable resource on which the House can draw.

Many overseas applicants appear to expect the University to be active in the provision of residential accommodation. The ready availability of good quality, reasonably affordable residential accommodation on-campus, suitable for the needs of students is therefore a significant contributor to the marketability of the University in international recruitment; as such, it needs to be actively managed as a factor contributing to the achievement of the University's strategic agenda.

Quite apart from the number of rooms a college or hall can offer, as a provider of residential accommodation it strengthens the University's status as a not-for-profit, student-focussed body. Consequently, the relationship between International House and the University of Sydney is of strategic importance in terms of the successful future of the House. A strong and open relationship will benefit the House in terms of marketing, ensure that the House will not be marginalised or isolated, and, indeed, guarantee that the House will be part of the University's plans for the future. If the University is to become truly international, with a campus and community of harmonious diversity, then IH needs to play a vital role. The House and the University together must adapt to the changes in the tertiary environment and provide an International House that will service the needs of its residents for many years to come.

Like all institutions in our rapidly changing world, then, IH is much concerned with consideration of the best ways of carrying on its mission in the new circumstances, which provide both challenges and opportunities. Whatever the outcome of these considerations, the future of IH remains bright. As ever, there is continuing opportunity for improvement in the standards of service, but overall, IH delivers acceptable value in terms of student accommodation, and the light of international fellowship and understanding continues to shine as strongly as always. Although internationalisation may have become part and parcel of university life, IH still offers something unique in providing the setting for different cultures to learn to understand each other and, we hope, value each other by living together. The need for such international understanding is, if anything, more crucial now than ever.

As has been true throughout its entire history, by far the most wonderful and remarkable aspect of IH is 'the light' that is generated and regenerated within the community of residents, term after term, year after year. And what is this light, symbolised each year in the Candlelight Ceremony? Slogan phrases such as 'international fellowship and understanding' are useful, but do not fully capture it. They are abstractions. The light is personal, as different and individual as each person is different and individual. The light involves a deeper appreciation that every person is a complex mix of influences (only some of which could be labelled 'national') combined with unique personal qualities. Year after year, since the very beginning, residents of IH have experienced this light. It is nurtured by living together within the IH community, by the gentle and unforced mixing that comes from the daily shared-table dining experience and by the program of activities. The House is a place of unexpected friendships and its light has altered the course of many lives.

Not every resident experiences the light to the same degree. Sometimes national or multinational cliques inhibit the possibility of external contact. Some residents prefer to be study hermits, keeping largely to themselves. But for the majority of residents and alumni, the light is sustained. This brings us to the *only* prediction that one can make in these concluding remarks: the light will be passed for as long as the IH community continues. Providing the setting to foster such a passing of the light remains the great challenge. The social, cultural and economic environments in which the House pursues its vision of international fellowship will continue to change. It is the vision that remains the same. The measure of our success as its current guardians will be how well we can equip the House to continue to adapt to the challenges of the next forty years, and beyond.

Sources

Publications:

I–House Life, International House, University of Chicago, USA, Autumn 2006/ Winter 2007 edition

Bernard Lillis (Executive Director, Finance and Administration, UTAS), *Financing the 'Experience of a Lifetime'*, AHAUCHI National Conference, Dunedin, 2006

Sharp Team Pty Ltd, *Appraisal* (paper on fund-raising), 2006

Appendix A

Chairpersons of Council, International House, University of Sydney, 1964–2007

1964	Lt-Gen. Sir John Northcott (Provisional Board of Management)	*1989*	Professor Hans Freeman
1965	Lt-Gen. Sir John Northcott (Provisional Board of Management)	*1990*	Professor Hans Freeman
		1991	Professor Hans Freeman
		1992	Dr Basil Voyagis
		1993	Dr Basil Voyagis
1966	Lt-Gen. Sir John Northcott	*1994*	Mr Brian Farmer
1967	Hon. Justice Charles McLelland	*1995*	Mr Brian Farmer
1968	Hon. Justice Charles McLelland	*1996*	Mr Brian Farmer
1969	Hon. Justice Charles McLelland	*1997*	Mr Dennis Cowdroy
1970	Hon. Justice Charles McLelland	*1998*	Mr Dennis Cowdroy
1971	Hon. Justice Charles McLelland	*1999*	Hon. Justice Dennis Cowdroy
1972	Emeritus Professor A. P. Elkin	*2000*	Mr Bruce Downie
1973	Emeritus Professor A. P. Elkin	*2001*	Mr Kenneth G. Coles
1974	Emeritus Professor A. P. Elkin	*2002*	Mr Kenneth G. Coles
1975	Emeritus Professor A. P. Elkin	*2003*	Mr Kenneth G. Coles
1976	Emeritus Professor A. P. Elkin	*2004*	Mrs Daphne Kok
1977	Emeritus Professor A. P. Elkin	*2005*	Mrs Daphne Kok
1978	Mr Ian G Hudson	*2006*	Mr David Shannon
1979	Mr Ian G Hudson	*2007*	Ms Denise North
1980	Mr Ian G Hudson		
1981	Hon. Justice David Mayer Selby		
1982	Hon. Justice David Mayer Selby		
1983	Hon. Justice David Mayer Selby		
1984	Miss Doreen Langley		
1985	Miss Doreen Langley		
1986	Miss Doreen Langley		
1987	Mr George Beattie Lean		
1988	Mr George Beattie Lean		

Appendix B

Fellows of International House, University of Sydney

Mrs Thelma Bate
Elected Fellow 1980

Sir Herman David Black
Elected Fellow 1980

Sir Nathaniel Bernard Freeman
Elected Fellow 1980

Dr Geoffrey Langford Howe
Elected Fellow 1980

Mr Wilson Harold Maze
Elected Fellow 1980

Mrs Rosalie McCutcheon
Elected Fellow 1980

Mrs Kathleen O'Neil
Elected Fellow 1980

Sir Harold Stanley Wyndham
Elected Fellow 1980

Dr Lauris Elms
Elected Fellow 1981

Miss Doreen Langley
Elected Fellow 1981

Mr Alex Dix
Elected Fellow 1981

Mrs Rosemary Berrick
Elected Fellow 1984

Mr Brian Farmer
Elected Fellow 1984

Ms Una Henderson
Elected Fellow 1984

Mr Robert Bland
Elected Fellow 1985

Mr Ian G. Hudson
Elected Fellow 1985

Ms Pauline Kennedy
Elected Fellow 1985

Mr Graeme de Graaff
Elected Fellow 1986

Ms Mollie Burns
Elected Fellow 1987

Mr George Lean
Elected Fellow 1989

Hon. Justice David Selby
Elected Fellow 1989

Mrs Renata Messerle
Elected Fellow 1991

Mrs Betty Boulton
Elected Fellow 1992

Professor Hans Freeman
Elected Fellow 1993

Mr Tim Beckett
Elected Fellow 1997

Dr Basil Voyagis
Elected Fellow 1997

Mr Geoffrey C. S. Andrews
Elected Fellow 1999

Hon. Justice Dennis Cowdroy
Elected Fellow 2000

Dr Toshiko Mori
Elected Fellow 2001

Mr Youngsok Song
Elected Fellow 2001

Mr Richard Wilson
Elected Fellow 2002

Mr Bruce Downie
Elected Fellow 2002

Mrs Gwen Ng
Elected Fellow 2002

Dr Richard Ng
Elected Fellow 2002

Dr Ruth Shatford
Elected Fellow 2002

Dr Joan Rowlands
Elected Fellow 2004

Mr Roger Wescombe
Elected Fellow 2006

Appendix C

Directors of International House

1965–1987	Graeme de Graaff
1987–1999	Geoffrey C. S. Andrews
1999–2002	Ruth Shatford
2002–present	Jessica Carroll
July 2005–June 2006	Keith Smith (Acting Director)

Appendix D

Chairpersons of International House Members' Association, 1967–2007

1967	Michael Hwang *(Terms 1 and 3)* Jone Tabaiwalu *(Term 2)*
1968	Robert Kuzelka *(until July)* Michael Rathgeber *(from July)*
1969	Percy Wong *(until June)* Rosamund Wood *(from July)*
1970	Grahame Kelly *(until June)* John Malcolm *(from July)*
1971	Trevor Allen
1972	Kow Idan
1973	Jennifer Mutton
1974	Lance Elliot
1975	Erica Sparks
1976	Greg Houseman
1977	Michael Johnson
1978	Neil Ackland
1979	Monique Doyle
1980	Benjamin Y. F. Fong
1981	Nicholas Stuart
1982	David Ho
1983	Charles Latimer
1984	Virginia Teodosio
1985	Richard Andrews
1986	Vishwanath Ramakrishnan
1987	George Roumeliotis
1988	Rico Liu
1989	Geoffrey Heenan
1990	Hazel Smith
1991	Melinda Penman
1992	Corinne Mann
1993	David Alexander
1994	Nimal Ratnesar
1995	Peter Revelant
1996	Vagira Abeysinghe
1997	Fang Yee Chee
1998	Nicholas Parslow
1999	Chaitanya Sharma
2000	Ekaterini Lymberopoulou
2001	Juan Camilo Reyes Hernandez
2002	Michelle Chalmers
2003	Jill Gambill
2004	Christopher Clarke
2005	Vinci Liu
2006	Nehal Kapadia
2007	Daniel Ackland

Appendix E

Presidents of Sydney University International House Alumni Association, 1969–2007

1969	Terence Birtles		*1999*	Toshiko Mori
1970	Terence Birtles		*2000*	Toshiko Mori
1971	George Rosier		*2001*	Joan Rowlands
1972	Frank Schaer		*2002*	Joan Rowlands
1973	Rosalie McCutcheon		*2003*	Joan Rowlands
1974	John Malcolm		*2004*	Nuli Lemoh
1975	Rosalie McCutcheon		*2005*	Nuli Lemoh
1976	David Shannon		*2006*	Nuli Lemoh
1977	Pauline Kennedy		*2007*	Christopher Moore
1978	Pauline Kennedy			
1979	Pauline Kennedy			
1980	Pauline Kennedy			
1981	Roger Wescombe			
1982	George Rosier			
1983	John Gascoigne			
1984	John Gascoigne			
1985	Benjamin Y. F. Fong			
1986	Nicholas Stuart			
1987	Pauline Kennedy			
1988	Pauline Kennedy			
1989	Gregory Bird			
1990	Gregory Bird			
1991	Geoffrey Heenan			
1992	Philayrath Phongsavan			
1993	Philayrath Phongsavan			
1994	Philayrath Phongsavan			
1995	Philayrath Phongsavan			
1996	Patricia McMahon			
1997	Patricia McMahon			
1998	Toshiko Mori			

Index

Page numbers in italics, e.g. *26,* refer to illustrations.